SKATEBOARDING IS NOT A CRIME

For Louise, whose skating
days are just beginning

BOOKS

THIS IS A CARLTON BOOK

First published by Carlton Books Limited in 1999

Copyright © 1999, 2004 Carlton Books Limited

10 9 8 7 6 5 4 3 2 1

A CIP catalogue record for this book is available
from the British Library.

ISBN 1 84442 663 7

Project Editor: Nigel Matheson
Project art direction: Jim Lockwood
Designer: Simon Osborne
Picture research: Stephen O'Kelly
Production: Lisa French

Printed and bound in Dubai

SKATEBOARDING IS NOT A CRIME

BOARD CULTURE PAST, PRESENT & FUTURE

James Davis with photographs by **Skin Phillips**

Contents

CHAPTER 1

CHAPTER 2

CHAPTER 3

CHAPTER 4

This book covers every aspect of skateboarding, from technical board development to the waves in popularity during the last half-century. Read about some of the greatest skateboarders who ever lived, and experience skateboard lifestyles all over the globe. The book is intended to be many things, not just a history. It is a guide book covering areas of skateboarding from tricks to terrain, skate art to skate video, determination to satisfaction, past to future. I hope that it will make you want to go out skateboarding, so perhaps it's a kind of self-help book, too. Dip in and out like a magazine, or just look at the great photography. Either way, have fun with it. If you discover just one thing that makes you love skating even more, then we have succeeded.

SKATEBOARDING IS EVERYTHING.
IT IS A PASTIME, A SPORT, A HOBBY.
A CRAZE, AN INDUSTRY AND A TOY.
A PROFESSION, AN EXCUSE, A GAME.
A LIFESTYLE, A DISTRACTION.
IT IS A REASON, NOT A CRIME.

The reason is why this book exists at all. If skateboarding means everything to you, then you need to ask why. If skateboarding means nothing to you, perhaps it soon will.
It has taken more than 50 years to get where we are today in skateboarding. This book is not just about those years, but the next 50 too. Consider this a halfway point. We have the opportunity to shape the future; we're holding it in our hands and we're riding it with our feet. Let's go…

1

History and Development

THERE IS NO OFFICIAL HISTORY OF SKATEBOARDING;
SKATEBOARDERS MAKE IT AS THEY ROLL ALONG. IF YOU
SKATE, YOU ARE A PART OF IT YOURSELF. BUT HOW DID
THE SKATEBOARD COME TO BE? THE INFLUENCES OF
SURFING AND ROLLER-SKATING ARE IMPORTANT, BUT
THEY PALE IN COMPARISON TO THE ENDLESS DESIRE OF
YOUNG PEOPLE TO CREATE THEIR OWN ENTERTAINMENT.
THIS PERFECTLY NATURAL ACTIVITY HAS PRODUCED
A MULTI-MILLION DOLLAR INDUSTRY, COUNTLESS TEARS,
PAIN AND BROKEN BONES, BUT ALSO IMMEASURABLE
AMOUNTS OF CHALLENGE, SATISFACTION AND, ABOVE
ALL, FUN FOR EVERYONE INVOLVED.

The Origins of Skateboarding

SKATEBOARDING is, of course, directly linked to surfing. But in many ways it is much more than that. Children throughout the ages have always found ways of playing around on wheeled objects of all kinds—from jumping on the back of horse-drawn carriages or delivery trolleys to fashioning go-kart-like constructions from just about anything they could get their hands on. The development we now call a skateboard is probably the inevitable result of centuries of insatiable fascination in young minds with anything that can be ridden on.

The fact that skateboarding is now (once again) both a massive sport and a hugely influential industry can be traced back to the lengthening of the teenage years—and the extended leisure time that went with that—which began in the 1950s. At that time, the youthful population was expanding rapidly and America was experiencing enormous social change. Before the Second World War, it was usual for young people to go straight into work after leaving school—college was only for better-off families.

Yet all this began to change after the War, and those in their teens began to develop a strong identity of their own. It's no surprise the word 'teenager' was coined at this time; the new social group had to be described somehow. These teenagers, with time, energy and a certain amount of money on their hands, were eager to create a new era. But this period was also a time of commercial innovation; the new, younger population needed toys to play with and things to do, so riches could be reaped by those who could capture the toy market with the latest craze, a classic example being Wham-O with the Hula Hoop in 1958.

As far as the connection with surfing goes, the origins of that sport lie with the tribal aristocracy and royalty who used to rule over the Hawaiian Islands. Yet their desires were similar in many ways to those of the modern skateboarder: to harness natural energy (the power of the ocean) for sport and, ultimately, pleasure. This can be directly compared with skateboarders, who harness the forces of gravity for the same reasons. As surfing in California grew massively in popularity among teenagers in the 1950s and 1960s, it became inevitable that any similar activity would enjoy comparable success. The stage was set.

Not that the skateboard's invention was an exact process—or even a quick

ABOVE:
**EARLY PIONEERS
ROAD-TEST THEIR BOARDS**

RIGHT:
**GARETH STEHR,
BACKSIDE FLIP**

one. The groundwork was laid decades earlier, with the invention and rise to popularity of the roller-skate. By the late 1930s, bored kids in the back alleys of America were beginning to take apart old roller-skates in search of better uses for them.

Scooters—a popular toy at the time—were an expensive option due to their bicycle-type wheels, but imaginative kids found a cheaper version could be improvised by fixing roller-skate undercarriages to a piece of wood—most likely a two-by-four—and nailing a wooden crate on to the front to be used for handlebars. These scooters were great fun, if a little dangerous due to their home-made nature, and many kids created variations on this theme using whatever stuff they could find.

A natural step for the bright-eyed youth of the time was to take the handlebars off—or let them fall off—and see if they could ride the board on its own. While it proved tricky to stay on for the length of a slope, it certainly saved the bother of having to keep nailing the handlebars back on when they fell off (usually at the same time as the rider). Of course, slopes and hills were just about all there was to skate. There were no purpose-built ramps of any kind, no concrete skateparks, and most flat areas were simply not smooth enough for the poor ride these early boards offered.

Around the late 1950s, open-minded Californian surfers began to realize that these new scooter-minus-the-handlebar contraptions were not just children's toys. The movement and balance needed to stay on one were similar to those required in surfing, so perhaps skating could be used as a kind of alternative to surfing on days when the waves were too flat. This moment of inspiration brought about a rapid change in the development of the skateboard, from crudely built toys to actual surfboards with wheels attached, and home-made decks specially carved into the shape of a surfboard.

These developments led directly to the first commercial production of a skateboard at the end of the 1950s.

Developments in Equipment

EARLY skateboards were almost entirely built at home, at least until companies such as Humco and Roller Derby introduced their first skateboards just before the 1960s. Even with the growth in popularity of the sport, the skateboard was still considered simply a toy until at least 1962 or 1963, when the surfing industry began to take a commercial interest. In 1963 the publisher of *Surf Guide*, Larry Stevenson, started up Makaha Skateboards, which was to be one of the first professional skateboard companies.

made another important breakthrough—the introduction of the kicktail. As well as providing better grip for the rider, it acted as a lever with which to lift and turn the skateboard with ease—an obvious enhancement that is now taken for granted, although few modern tricks are possible without a kicktail and nose. Larry actually obtained a patent for his idea, although it later proved impossible for him to collect royalties on the kicktail's incorporation by other manufacturers.

Because early decks were not laminated, they had little flexibility, or 'flex'

as it is now known. Activities such as the slalom, which was a huge part of skateboarding in the early years, required decks with a quick, interactive response in order to aid the rider to turn several times per second.

Larry Gordon, from surfboard company Gordon and Smith, introduced the Fiberflex skateboard around the latter part of 1964. Its laminated deck featured a composite of wood and fiberglass which proved amazingly responsive. The curve of the deck had a kind of memory and, when pushed out of place, it returned to its original state. All skateboard decks these days feature this kind of flex to some extent.

It took the innovations and investment of the second phase of skateboarding (from the early to late 1970s) before deck manufacturers began to use the construction technique that is still in place today.

RIGHT:
LINDSEY ROBERTSON, DOUBLE SET OLLIE
BELOW:
PETER RAMONDETTA, FEEBLE GRIND

DECKS: FROM OAK TO ALUMINUM AND BEYOND

Skateboard decks were usually made from wood, often just solid pieces of oak, although it wasn't long before companies began to introduce all sorts of different materials, from fiberglass to foam, plastic to aluminum. The size and shape of decks has also changed continuously, not only through trial and error, but through the needs of different types of skaters.

Downhill riders wanted longer, wider, more stable boards; freestylers and slalom skaters needed shorter boards for their quicker response; pool skaters needed a combination of the two; and more recent vertical and street skaters have needed precise dimensions in order to perfect their incredibly difficult tricks.

In the late 1960s, Larry Stevenson

**DAVE SMITH,
SMITH GRIND**

Canadian skateboarder Willi Winkel worked together with the Sims company to produce the first decks laminated entirely with maple. The boards were incredibly popular, and before long many other manufacturers were using the same idea. With the gradual introduction of a concave profile and the eventual decision to use seven veneers of maple, the resulting combination of strength, low weight and flex has yet to beaten.

It has taken a lot of refinement since the late 1970s to produce the decks used nowadays. The veneers of the deck are much thinner now, and the glue used to join them has improved vastly. In the mid-1980s decks came in all sorts of shapes, and lots of experimentation took place, often in the name of marketing: wavy-edged decks; asymmetric, foot-shaped decks; fishtails; and decks with side protrusions for mid-air grabbing.

In the late 1980s, Powell Peralta introduced the Boneite series; these composite constructions offered much greater strength with only a slight increase in weight, although they failed to catch on in the long term. Santa Cruz released the ground-breaking Everslick boards in 1989, featuring a special, ultra-thin type of plastic covering the bottom of the deck—perfect for sliding across almost any surface. Coming at a time when skateboarders were beginning to tire of the extra weight added by accessories such as rails and tail-savers, the introduction of Everslick helped to speed up the elimination of such plastic extras—at least by most street skaters—thus paving the way for a higher level of board control and trick complexity.

Companies experimented once again in the late 1990s with different ply constructions, from five to nine layers, although by this time most decks were largely indistinguishable, apart from the graphics and any obvious size or concave differences. A few companies continued to experiment with different techniques and materials, notably Flip's New Wave Construction which featured corrugated stiffening ribs across the length of the board, but no truly major breakthroughs have been made since maple lamination.

WHEELS: FROM METAL TO URETHANE

Skateboard wheels have come a long way since the metal 'bone-shakers' used in the early 1960s. Not only did metal wheels give an uncomfortable ride, but they offered little grip and were prone to

rust, particularly in the coastal resorts where most skaters of the day were to be found. Metal was soon replaced by the slightly better alternative of clay, coupled with loose ball-bearings. Although the ride was smoother and faster, grip was still a major problem, the clay wore out quickly and loose bearings were prone to escape. It was the introduction of urethane wheels in the early 1970s that truly revolutionized the market and helped to kick-start the second popular phase of skateboarding history.

A surfer named Frank Nasworthy brought the idea of urethane skateboard wheels to fruition with his Cadillac Wheel in 1973. He had to drive around Californian surf shops himself in order to sell them, but the wheels quickly became a success once skateboarders appreciated what a vast improvement they offered. Nearly two years later, NHS produced the Road Rider 2 wheel. This was the first skateboard wheel to feature 608 precision bearings and forever stamped out the need to assemble loose ball-bearings individually when putting together a skateboard.

The introduction of urethane along with aircraft-precision bearings was instrumental in allowing skateboarders greater creativity in their riding: skaters could now go much faster, which also meant much higher jumps, and places such as empty swimming-pools could be truly conquered.

Since that time, wheel compounds have hardened to cope with new terrain and techniques, and various improvements have been made in the design and construction. Wheels with double-radius edges were introduced by George Powell, of Powell Corporation, in 1977. The rounded edges of these wheels made many of the tricks much easier as they increased the wheel's ability to roll over a variety of surfaces and planes. This innovation has since become a standard feature.

Throughout the 1990s, the core of the wheel was undergoing continual innovation. Stiffer cores, made of

RIGHT:

**CASWELL BERRY,
BLUNTSLIDE**

improved urethane compounds or other materials, were used to provide greater stability for the bearings and offered still faster speeds. Full precision-shielded or sealed bearings became the standard and were made of very high-quality steel. New types of urethane were continually developed to offer better rebound, and the incredibly complicated process and refinement of wheel-making continues to improve to this day.

TRUCKS: FROM CHEAP TOYS TO COMPLEX GEOMETRY

The Chicago Roller Skate Company patented their roller-skate truck in 1935. It was a ground-breaking design at the time, and one on which skateboard trucks are still loosely based. Skateboarders had to go on buying and using variations on the roller-skate truck right up until the mid-1970s, when several skateboard truck manufacturers started up; such as Tracker, Bennett, Gullwing and Ermico Enterprises. The roller-skate trucks these new companies wished to improve upon were pretty hopeless for skateboarding and created numerous problems: as well as being too weak to cope with many of the

newest tricks, the kingpin (the main bolt which provides the axis of the truck) stuck out above the top and scraped across uneven ground.

In addition, the truck itself was very poor at turning because roller-skates had very different design needs in this area. Another annoying aspect was that roller-skate trucks came with a variety of different mounting-hole patterns—this meant the skateboard deck had to be drilled by the skater themselves once they got it home. Inevitably, teenagers cut corners (as well as fingers) when drilling the holes to screw the trucks on, and the trucks were often misaligned—resulting in a skateboard that didn't go in a straight line.

The first skateboard truck to combat the kingpin problem came from Bennett in 1975, and was called the Bennett Hijacker. This immediately proved popular and sold in thousands, but the baseplate of the truck was still too weak.

Tracker were the first to produce a standardized four-hole layout on a stronger baseplate, also in 1975. This layout was to be followed by most truck manufacturers right up until the early 1990s, when the outer holes were moved slightly into the truck to reduce the chance of the mounting bolts getting caught during tricks such as nose and tail-slides.

Both Gullwing and Ermico Enterprises worked hard at addressing the turning problems associated with roller-skate trucks. Ermico's first truck, called the Stroker, was very maneuver-able, if a bit heavy and expensive. By 1978 they had introduced the Independent truck, which was widely imitated and of which a much-refined version is still produced today by Independent Truck Co.

Most other developments in truck design were part of a natural progression established by those early leaders, although Z made the rather interesting Z-Roller truck, which featured a spinning cylinder around the axle to assist with grinds and was still being sold in the late 1990s. Materials such as brass, plastic, magnesium and steel have all been used as ingredients in truck-making, but manufacturers have now settled on aluminum as the primary ingredient.

Companies such as Grind King, Venture and Thunder continued to beaver away at improving the overall geometry and performance of trucks throughout the 1980s and 1990s.

Nowadays trucks are required to be enormously strong, as well as light, reliable and maneuverable, and numerous new truck-specific companies have sprung up. In the 1990s names such as Royal, Fury, Destructo, Mercury, Orion, Krux, Jones and Webb each refined the basic concepts of truck design even further—from the exact positioning of the axle to the nature of the pivoting mechanism—on the long, slow path to creating the perfect truck. In 2003, Softrucks introduced the Softrucks Practice Truck, a wheel-less soft undercarriage designed specifically for practicing maneuvers—at 0 mph—at home.

MIKE FRAIER,
FAKIE VARIAL 540

Shoes and
Safety Equipment

IT'S hard to believe now, but the earliest skateboarders didn't wear shoes when they went skating. It was just assumed—perhaps from the connection with surfing—that you had to go barefoot. But it wasn't too long before legions of scarred and bloody feet sent an obvious message to their owners: streets are not made of water. The sports shoe industry was then in its infancy, so low-top sailing shoes or Converse Chuck Taylors offered about the best protection for the feet while still giving a feeling of flexibility.

In 1966 Vans released their first sneakers: strong, flexible and grippy, they proved perfect for skateboarding. It was the start of an amazing success story for the company, and by the turn of the Millennium, Vans was one of the most popular brands of sports shoe in the world.

There were no more major developments in skate shoes until the mid-1980s, when the sneaker construction of the time began to prove inadequate for the innovations in tricks and techniques which were beginning to occur. Skaters required a much greater standard of durability and cushioning—particularly with moves like the ollie—and this was provided by a new company: Airwalk.

This company worked closely with skateboarders to address the specific problems other shoes had, and the results were very successful. By the time Airwalks had become a fashion item outside of skateboarding in the early 1990s, some new runners had entered the race—Vision and Etnies continued to develop new durability and cushioning

RIGHT:
FRONTSIDE CROOKS

LEFT:
FRANK HIRATA, OLLIE GRAB, OCEANSIDE, CA

MARK GONZALES, NOSESLIDE

concepts, and Etnies released the first ever signature-model skateboard shoe: the Natas Kaupas. The huge success of this shoe set the pace for the rest of the decade, and today signature models are a standard element of most skate shoe companies' lines. In fact, many pro skaters earn far more from sales of their shoe than from anything else. Highly advanced technology is beginning to be used in the products; with the three main areas to address being grip, cushioning and durability, countless formulae of rubbers, polyurethanes, vinyls and gels are tried and tested in an effort to improve the qualities of the shoe. The market is now enormous, and with only around 5 per cent of skate shoes being sold to skaters in 2003, hasn't gone unnoticed by major shoe corporations such as Nike, adidas and Puma who have all released skateboard-specific shoe ranges. Nike produced an eye-opening marketing campaign which featured athletes from more mainstream sports being discriminated against in the

same way that skateboarders had been. This campaign did a lot to teach non-skaters from all walks of life about the specific problems associated with the sport, and perhaps in many ways helped open the floodgates of corporate cash that was beginning to stream through the industry. Adidas had success with two signings, Mark Gonzales and Lance Mountain, both of whom were legendary skaters from the previous two decades, and, deservedly, had well-designed shoes named after them.

Skateboard shoe construction is still advancing at a rapid rate. Ideas have been adapted from other sports shoes and research and development is now a hugely important part of most companies' long-term planning.

It's important to remember that skateboard sneakers were once considered safety devices, and perhaps should be even more so today. If the edges of the sole are designed badly, or an air bubble bursts, ankle and heel injuries can result.

Other safety devices such as helmets, knee and elbow pads, gloves, wrist guards and hip pads have been gradually introduced and developed since the mid-1960s. Safety gear is an important item for those learning to skate, as well as for more advanced riders. Before the advent of dedicated equipment, skaters used thin elbow and knee pads taken from any other sport that used them, from basketball to motorcycling. These proved inadequate for the specific types of fall associated with skateboarding and, instead, led to one of the most important product breakthroughs in the late 1970s.

Plastic caps were added to bulky style knee pads by companies such as Rector, and revolutionized the well-practised art of falling off a skateboard: the lack of friction associated with these hardened caps proved perfect for sliding down the surfaces of ramps and pools. This meant that skateboarders simply had to slide on to their knees while wearing the pads to escape more serious injury. A positive side-effect of this innovation was that more daredevil moves could be attempted with less danger to the skater, and this more aggressive style of skating helped push tricks even further up more nearly-vertical terrain.

Many different sporting activities require the use of helmets, so skateboarders bought or borrowed them from all sorts of different disciplines.

Indeed it was some time before manufacturers began marketing helmets specifically at skateboarders, and even longer before they produced helmets aimed directly at them.

There are several helmet standards to which companies adhere, such as ATSM, CPSC, CE and Snell. ATSM was the only one which offered a standard directed at skateboarding helmets by the late 1990s, although the other standards covered similar activities. The best advice for skateboarders has always been to buy certified helmets with a good fit and a good reputation, always check with your skate shop for details.

All-Terrain Vehicles

WHEN the first skateboarders rode their rickety contraptions through the streets and back alleys of America, little did they realize that 40 years later their successors would be riding directly up the vertical walls that surrounded them. Such has been the pace of change. The evolution of tricks and terrain has seen skateboarders go from only the smoothest, easiest path available to the hardest, most-challenging terrain and techniques imaginable. It has been a long and winding road, to say the least.

Early riders ventured out into the schoolyards of California, which featured smoothly banked slopes around the edges. These wave-like obstacles were obviously perfect to try to recreate some of the popular surfing moves of the time. Often these just involved changing foot position on the board, carving around in a giant sweep or dragging the rear hand as if through water. More dynamic tricks were quickly discovered by imaginative early skaters such as Torger Johnson, Danny Bearer and John Freis.

The introduction of the kicktail in the late 1960s made some of the early tricks much easier, as well as bringing in a whole slew of new moves.

Skateboarders would place empty drinks cans halfway up the banks and weave in and out of them, while others sought out large hills down which to attempt survival on a skateboard. There were certainly no aerial or flipping moves at this stage; even with the imagination to try and invent them, skaters might well have been thwarted by the poor equipment.

BELOW:
A SKATE ROAD TRIP

Most people point to skater Gary Swanson as the first to ride an empty swimming pool, around 1963. After staying on a low carve around the deep end, it is unlikely that he could imagine the possibilities that would later be uncovered around the blue tiles of the pool and beyond.

As contests began to be organized, slalom became a staple aspect of the sport. Mellow sloping ramps were sometimes constructed on which to hold the slalom competitions. Long-jumping and high-jumping also became popular—their very measurability allowed everyone to see who was the best.

A move made possible only by bare-foot skating was the Gorilla Grip: the toes of each foot were painfully grasped around the nose and tail of the board and then the rider jumped and sometimes turned in the air with the board attached to his feet.

Empty pools weren't properly skated until the mid-1970s, when new equipment allowed the bravest skaters to carve up to the blue tiles. With wider trucks, the coping of the pool could be ground at the peak of the turn by a few talented riders. A natural development was for the skateboarder to fly into the air above the coping while grabbing the board, turning around and re-entering the pool. Moves like this were favored by more aggressively styled skaters such as Tony Alva, Jay Adams and Stacy Peralta, who were pushing back established skateboarding boundaries for Dogtown, and whose stories would be told 30 years later in *Dogtown: The Movie*.

The first purpose-built skateparks were constructed in the late 1960s and early 1970s, but these offered little challenge or excitement. It took the investment of the commercial sector in the mid-1970s and the more modern parks that followed, to transform that part of the industry.

The first generation of commercially built parks, such as those in Daytona, Florida and Carlsbad, California, were still rather poorly designed, and neglected the needs of users such as pool skaters. However, the construction of parks was proving to be a big business, and was generally considered to be one of the most profitable opportunities of the time.

There were several advantages to skating in the parks. Primarily, they provided a safer environment for younger skaters to learn in, but as the terrain improved and better designs were implemented, new tricks could be developed and replicated on the more reliable terrain.

The second wave of parks, which came a couple of years later, was much better-designed. Skaters often had an input during the early stages, and this resulted in some of the most legendary parks ever built. Probably the most notable of these was Upland's Pipeline skatepark with its infamous Combi-Pool, later recreated in the first of a new generation of Vans skateparks, opening in Orange County, California in late 1999.

The most notable new trick to come from the 1970s, and probably the most important trick in modern skateboarding today, was the ollie. Alan 'Ollie' Gelfand pioneered this technique of getting the board into the air without gripping it with the hands or feet in the late 1970s. First of all it was developed above the lip in the concrete parks, later on ramps, and finally, by the early 1980s, a street version was perfected. Since that time, most street tricks have been based around the move, and it is an essential stepping stone to be crossed in the life of a young skater.

By the end of the 1970s, many of the concrete parks were beginning to close due to financial difficulties. Insurance premiums were rising with the perceived increase in the danger of the sport, and someone had to pay. The tremendous outlay required to build the parks had also proved very difficult to repay, and with admission or membership fees rising because of these factors, skaters once again took their search for the ultimate spot elsewhere. This undoubtedly meant that streets and schoolyards were revisited once more, although this time the developments in skateboarding trickery over the previous five or ten years meant a whole new set of challenges were presented.

Freestyle (flatground trick) skaters began to find ways of adopting some of the vert-oriented moves to the street. One of the earliest pioneers of this way of thinking was Steve Rocco, who transfered moves like handplants to curbs and street corners. At the same time, skaters who loved the vertical experience were looking to recreate it with the construction of wooden ramps.

Newer vertical moves involved more of a straight-up-and-down trajectory, so tall, thinner ramps proved perfectly adequate for these and many more tricks. A flat bottom was also added to ramps at this time: skaters who were traveling increasingly fast realized the need to have more time to prepare for the next wall.

Street skating began to explode in popularity and was hailed by some forward-looking industry types as the future of skateboarding. Early street contests were held with obstacles such as cars, traffic cones and steeper wooden banks to fly out of. The ollie was beginning to come of age with the incredible skills of skaters like Mark Gonzales and Natas Kaupas, who not only pushed it much higher into the air, but took it across gaps, down steps and combined it with freestyle moves such as kickflips. Street skaters were now taking inspiration from both vertical skating and freestyle skating, combining moves and taking them to fresh new obstacles. Mark Gonzales was the first to slide down a handrail around 1987 and this daredevil step forward ushered in the modern era of street skating, combining technique with significant levels of risk.

Vertical skating had begun to enjoy a comeback, and ramp designs were crafted in ever more complex ways. The ramp built by Tim Payne for Powell Peralta's third video, *The Search for Animal Chin*, was the most ground-breaking of its time. Featuring multiple transitions, planes and surfaces, it allowed the highly talented Bones Brigade team members to innovate in

were skating switch or not—the clique of skateboarding was further established by the increased education required to appreciate a skaters tricks. Mostly, though, it was all about challenge, and before too long kids who were just learning to skate began to disregard labels such as regular and goofy foot, and tried to learn all tricks both ways.

Switchstance rapidly crossed over to vert skating along with some of the more modern tricks such as ollie kickflips, through innovators such as Mike Crum, Colin McKay and Danny Way. Older moves, such as handplants and fastplants, began to phase out on the ramps as these new challenges arrived.

On the streets things got even more technical with a to return to the roots of freestyle with slow-moving, multiple-spinning tricks. This phase produced a counter-movement, however, and it didn't take too long before skaters were concentrating on taking simpler tricks such as ollies and grinds to their natural extremes. The 1990s and 2000s saw death-defying ollies and grinds down massive drops and handrails from some of the sport's biggest names—Pat Duffy, Jamie Thomas, Chad Muska and Geoff Rowley, to name a few.

Around that period concrete parks made a comeback, this time mainly from the public sector, whose liability worries were removed when skateboarding eventually became classified as a hazardous sport in the US, thus resolving insurance issues at a stroke.

In 2004, the Skate Plaza concept began to to take off with the first purpose -built park in Kettering, Ohio, the home of creator and DC pro Rob Dyrdek. Rob had imagined a new era of skateparks that were designed and built to look like actual town plazas, featuring trees and plants and patches of grass amongst the steps, ledges, benches and drops. Only time would yet tell if this concept could be realised effectively, but there was much support for the idea from both the skate industry and city planners.

ways previously unimaginable. This new standard in ramp design also allowed vert skaters to begin feeding off the bold new moves of street skaters—and vice versa—and the evolution of variations in tricks sped up once again.

The next major development came up from the streets a few years later, again from the likes of Mark Gonzales, and pushed later by Salman Agah.

Gonzales began to use his front foot on the nose of his board to perform tricks that were normally done with his back foot on the tail. This was equivalent to writing with the wrong hand, and this strange, difficult-to-comprehend style of skating later became known as switchstance. The whole point was to try and do tricks in direct opposition to the norm for the rider; thus, if you were goofy-footed, you could try and ollie regular-footed.

This new technique doubled the amount of tricks you could do on a skateboard overnight, although the challenge was immense. Another big part of the appeal was that only fellow-skaters could recognize if you

ABOVE:
MATT MUMFORD,
STALEFISH

Tony Hawk

TONY HAWK is the most famous name in skateboarding, and for good reason. He has won more contests, skated more consistently and acted more professionally than any other skateboarder alive. From his early beginnings in the concrete parks of California, Tony Hawk dominated vert skating throughout the 1980s and 1990s. He's also starred in the movies, had a series of video games named after him, co-owned a successful skate company, featured in the famous 'Got Milk?' ad campaign and is now the face of McDonald's—there can't be much left for him to do.

Waves of Devotion

JERON WILSON,
HALF CAB INTO
JUMP RAMP

SKATEBOARDING has long been regarded as a fad, and its rises and falls in popularity have done little to help shake off this label. Often forced into the same bracket as hula-hoops, yo-yos, Frisbees and milk-caps, companies have jumped on and off the bandwagon as they saw fit. But skateboarding has come on in leaps and bounds since the 1950s, mainly through the commitment put in by the skaters and a handful of companies that have remained supportive when things got tough. Today's success proves that it was only the short-sighted misers that labeled skateboarding a fad.

The economic climate in America at the birth of skateboarding was one of social upheaval. New gadgets were introduced every day, for the home, the office, the car or the children. It was inevitable that the first skateboards would be seen as a craze during their introduction at the end of the 1950s. While the activity boomed and many new companies sprang up, it was short-lived, almost dying-out completely by 1965. There were several main causes for this: the standard of boards was so poor that many accidents were caused simply through equipment failure—bearings fell out, wheels fell off and trucks didn't turn. The rise in the accident rate concerned police and authorities at a national level.

Many concerned organisations tried to have skateboarding banned altogether, while city authorities introduced local bans in downtown districts. Commercially, manufacturers overestimated the number of skate-boards they could sell, or shops simply ordered too many; either way, warehouses were piled high with boards that couldn't be shifted, causing many firms to go out of business.

In just a few short years, a whole industry complete with magazines (*The Quarterly Skateboarder*), manufacturers, distributors, shops and millions of consumers had risen from nothing—the first crash was almost inevitably provoked by this far-too-rapid growth. The next few years were lean on the business side, but the skaters kept going and it gave those who loved the sport a chance to take a breath and see where they could go to next.

The next phase came directly after the introduction of the urethane wheel in 1973. With the improvements in both speed and safety offered by the new wheels, coupled with precision bearings, kids could once more enjoy the delights of the skateboard. Those who had kept going during the underground years amazed all the new entrants with the dazzling array of tricks that had been created, and once again a multi-million-dollar industry started up. *The Quarterly Skateboarder* enjoyed a successful return as *Skateboarder Magazine*, and skateboarding became a world-wide sport.

The new skateparks held massive contests that were often featured on television, and major corporations such as Pepsi had their own skateboard teams. At the end of the decade, optimistic organizers hoped to get skateboarding entered as a sport in the

thinnest decks and the smallest wheels. The very short life-span of these products was capitalized upon by some companies, who released lighter but weaker equipment in the knowledge that short-term profits would prosper. Coupled with this was the arrival of a new competitor—rollerblading. Fickle youths chose rollerblading in droves, and left the '1980s' sport of skateboarding behind.

The new worldwide community that had developed in skating was strong in many ways, but also prone to global financial issues like most other industries. The recession of this time finished off many companies and pushed skateboarding into a lull for a couple of years. This low point was not, however, as clearly defined and hard-hitting as those of the late 1960s and late 1970s. Internally, the sport grew from strength to strength, and the skateboard community carried on holding yearly world championship contests in Münster, Germany, moving a few dozen kilometers to Dortmund in 1999.

Two new magazines were published in 1992, reflecting the ever-widening scope of potential readers. *Big Brother* set out to bring the enjoyment back to skateboarding and the established industry, and provide suitably controversial content. This supposedly negative magazine actually had a very positive effect—some of the companies it had provoked quickly changed their acts for the better, and helped put the fun back into skating. The other new magazine, *Slap*, provided yet another viewpoint on the expanding sport.

As skateboarding became more popular, so many of the older companies began to develop a much more long-term outlook.

The singularly urgent need to try and prevent skateboarding from going under again, while still retaining its unique identity was recognized. Product research and development became an important concern once more, as did aspects of management such as looking after team members properly. The World Cup

Skateboarding (WCS) organization, formed from the ashes of the NSA in 1994, took over administration of many worldwide events. It also provided rankings for professionals based on the points accumulated by those who had entered its contests. Major corporations took an interest in skateboarding once again, and the sport featured in food, car, clothing and watch commercials. By the late 1990s, watch and sunglass companies were signing up skateboard teams. Casio, in particular, featured models with designs by Ed Templeton.

ABOVE:
BLAKE CONVEY, PADDINGTON

LEFT:
CHAD MUSKA, BACKSIDE 50-50

The mood in the industry at the beginning of the new century was very positive.

A wide range of companies and magazines had been established to cater for every type of skater; older forms of skateboarding such as longboarding were making a comeback and a large number of the top skaters were earning more than enough money to live on. With no perceived threats on the horizon, the future looked bright for skateboarders around the globe.

Eric Koston

MANY skaters believe Eric Koston can do just about any street trick there is; he can certainly do more than nearly every other skater alive, and his amazing talents have earned him a place among the very top pros in skateboarding history. His relaxed style is inspiring to watch, as he makes the most difficult tricks seem effortless. He has also set new standards in professionalism, remaining loyal to a few sponsors for longer than most, and traveling constantly in the name of doing his job as best he can, while having as much fun as possible along the way.

The Global Skate Village

SKATEBOARDING BECAME A TRULY GLOBAL PHENOMENON IN THE LATE 1970S, WITH ITS ENORMOUS POPULARITY AND WORLDWIDE COVERAGE. THOSE EARLY, HECTIC DAYS SPARKED-OFF SKATE SCENES IN COUNTLESS COUNTRIES, AND THE PROCESS OF GLOBALIZATION BEGAN. COUNTRIES LIKE CANADA, BRAZIL, GREAT BRITAIN AND AUSTRALIA QUICKLY DEVELOPED SKATE INDUSTRIES OF THEIR OWN, WHICH ARE STILL GOING STRONG TODAY. THE US HAS REMAINED THE DOMINANT FORCE IN SKATEBOARDING, BUT FOREIGN SKATERS AND COMPANIES HAVE CONTINUALLY SHOWN UP ON CALIFORNIAN SHORES AND UPSET THE APPLE-CART.

USA

TOP:
**JOHN CARDIEL,
BACKSIDE GRAB**

ABOVE:
**KENNY HUGHES,
BACKSIDE TAILSLIDE**

THERE'S no doubt that America is the home of skateboarding: spiritually, culturally, physically, whichever way you look at it. The West Coast in particular has the climate, architecture, history and people to continually influence skate-related events across the world, whether it's new board technologies, trick, spot or clothing fashions, they often come from somewhere in California.

Skating spread quickly across the States in the 1970s, when improved equipment allowed more skaters to enjoy this previously surf community-led sport. Strong scenes built up in New York, Philadelphia, Chicago, Dallas and so on, creating a buzz that pulsed across the nation spreading the four-wheeled message to the smaller towns, and sewing the seeds of a migration that still occurs today:- the exodus of many amateur skaters from all parts towards California in order to make their name.

At one point this migration was necessary if you wanted to make skating your career, now it is less so, but is still a considered option for many, at least on a temporary basis. As the spots of Los Angeles and San Francisco slowly dry up, the necessity to be seen skating there diminishes. A culture that demands freshness prefers to see skaters in newer locations, smaller towns, unknown and foreign spots are becoming the young star's stage of choice. Skating in the US will always be a dream for many, and is worth a visit at least once in every skater's lifetime.

The rest of this book covers the specfics of American skate history and skate scenes today, so let's move north to begin our global skate trip.

ABOVE:
**MATT HENSLEY,
TAILSLIDE**

RIGHT:
**COLT CANNON,
NOSEPICK**

Canada

Canada is big enough for there to be an East-West divide in the skate scene, but it has little to do with rivalry and competition and more to do with significant weather differences. Parts of the east have six- or eight-month winters, and this means skateboarding is only appreciated and frantically executed during the all-too-brief summer months. Meanwhile, in the western regions such as British Columbia, a milder weather system and an abundance of concrete parks create an amazing environment for skateboarding. It took a lot of skater organization as well as some surprising help from the authorities to get these parks built. Places like the Whistler bowls are recognized as being some of the best concrete parks in the world. Those parks, as well as cities such as Vancouver in the West and Toronto in the East, are essential stops on the global skate traveler's itinerary.

By the late 1990s, a Canadian video magazine in the style of 411 called Skate Canada had been established. As well as showcasing fresh talent coming out of the country, the videos focused on some of the areas usually ignored by the American media, such as Quebec, and opened countless eyes to talented skateboarders in those parts.

Shops such as Red Dragons and the Rick McCrank-owned Antisocial in Vancouver have proved that the Canadian scene continues to grow and succeed, providing suitably alternative products for Canadian youth to save up for and buy.

Red Dragons was named after a group of skaters who hung out and skated together—a tightly knit group, their combined skate talent was massive. Influential skaters like Rick Howard, Colin McKay and Moses Itkonen developed much of their skill on the streets and skateparks of western Canada, and this environment continues to create exceptional skaters. More recently, Rick McCrank and Alex Chalmers made heads turn, and skaters all over the world realized that Canadian skateboarding remains a force to be reckoned with.

THE skate scene in Canada has frequently been overlooked. While the influence of their US neighbors is pervasive, Canadian skaters often take a more individual approach. Innovators like Willi Winkel, a skater and businessman in the 1970s and 1980s, helped to carve an early path through the American industry, at a time when skateboarders were desperate for advanced equipment to help them create the newest tricks.

Skull Skates is another of the most important companies to have come out of Canada. They moved from Vancouver to California and back again, while producing some truly influential graphics and boards like the Hosoi 'Hammerhead' model. They were also famed for their innovative work with the rock industry, producing boards for bands such as the Red Hot Chili Peppers.

In the 1980s, Canadian freestyler Kevin Harris made it as a member of the Bones Brigade, Powell Peralta's legendary team.

Kevin later set up one of the most innovative skateparks to be made out of wood—inspired by the Animal Chin ramp—the influence of which can still be seen today through its use of multi-level ramps and the huge variety of possible lines.

ABOVE:
**JASON LEE,
GAP TO 50-50**

RIGHT:
**CASWELL BERRY,
NOSEGRIND**

South America

SKATING in this continent is an extremely varied activity, depending on which region you visit. The scene in Brazil has always been huge, and since the 1970s the country has had its own skate industry.

This was due partly to the restricted economy, and partly to the abundance of raw materials. Deck companies started up by the dozen, in the knowledge that domestically produced equipment would be a lot cheaper for the skaters to buy than imported US product.

By 1993, skateboarding was the fourth most popular youth activity in the country after surfing, volleyball and soccer, according to a poll conducted by a national radio station.

Skateboarding is traditionally centered around the major cities such as São Paulo and Rio de Janeiro, although countless smaller towns and cities have thriving scenes too.

Brazil's dangerous traffic and poorly constructed urban streets have meant that skaters often had to grow up skating in the concrete parks. However, this has been no bad thing—there are probably more concrete parks in Brazil than any other country, and they range from tightly transitioned 1970s parks to smooth, ultra-modern 1990s master-pieces. Most of the parks are also public, and therefore free to skate. Places like the São Caetano cement bowls in São Paulo and the Rio Sul bowl in Rio de Janeiro are among the world's best.

While Brazil is most famous in the sporting world for its soccer players, the immense popularity of activities like skateboarding has also produced several world-wide names over the years. Skaters such as Lincoln Ueda,

LEFT:
**ERIC KOSTON,
SWITCH TAILSLIDE**

ABOVE:
GERSHON MOSELEY,
SWITCH CROOKED GRIND

LEFT:
MATT MUMFORD,
BACKSIDE SMITH

Rodil Menezes, Rodil de Araujo, Bob Burnquist and Rodrigo Texeira have traveled the world in pursuit of contest victories, and are treated as national heroes back home.

Magazines like *Tribo*, *Overall* and *100% Skate* have covered skating throughout the country, including details of Brazil's well-established contest series. Skating has even reached places like Ecuador; a couple of parks were built in the 1970s in places such as the capital, Quito, but never really took-off because of the huge expense of importing boards from America.

However, by around 1988, street skating took off and a few surf shops in the biggest city, Guayaquil, began selling boards. Of course, the import rates and the low incomes of most families meant they were still an expensive proposition. If a younger skater broke their board, they would often assume that their skating days were over.

Skaters usually go out after five in the evening, because of the heat, and when the streets and shopping centers are theirs to explore. Because the police often have far more serious crimes to deal with skaters are, for the most part, left alone.

Nowadays, an organization called GQUIL runs the skating in Ecuador. They organize events and build ramps when and where they can, and provide a legitimate framework in which Ecuador's poorer kids can enjoy themselves in a positive way.

Elsewhere in South America, the skate scenes vary enormously from country to country.

Street skating has grown massively in places like Argentina, whereas much poorer countries such as Colombia are just beginning to accept skateboarding as a possible youth activity, mainly due to some high-profile demonstrations put on by visiting US pros.

Australia, New Zealand and South Africa

AUSTRALIA has one of the best-developed skate scenes outside the United States. With a strong surfing environment, a large, young population and an abundance of space, the Australian authorities have rarely hesitated to provide skateboarding facilities since as far back as the late 1970s.

The acceptance of skateboarding as a legitimate youth activity was reflected in 1990, when an Australian postal stamp was issued featuring vert skaters.

The country has remained a favorite stop for pro skaters from around the world, many of whom have influenced the skate scene and in turn often been influenced themselves by the friendly and relaxed attitude of many Australian skaters.

By the late 1990s, Aussies Chad Bartie, Matt Mumford, Morgan Campbell, Wade Burkitt and brothers Tas and Ben Pappas had all achieved international fame through their skateboarding talents. Back in Australia, countless other skaters pushed the limits of what was possible on the concrete parks, and helped to build a strong national industry.

From the older parks such as Fish Ponds and Nunwading in Melbourne to the newer places like Wollongong near Sydney and Belconnel in Canberra, skaters have an amazing variety of spots to choose from.

Ramps have frequently been built on the Sydney beachfronts such as Bondi and Manly, while over in isolated Perth a solid street scene coexists with the close-knit surfing community.

Skaters around the world may remember the famous Cockroach wheels which originated in Australia at the beginning of the 1990s—they featured a row of black roaches printed on to the running surface. Companies like Time and magazines such as *Slam*, *Skatin' Life*, *Australian Skateboarding* and *Speed Wheels* have helped provide the impetus for a successful Antipodean skate industry over many years.

New Zealand sees less frequent visits from touring skaters, but still contains a historic selection of concrete parks built in the 1970s and 1980s, such as Lynnfield and New Lynn, which were often frequented by 1980s legend

ABOVE:
CARL SHIPMAN,
FRONTSIDE BLUNTSLIDE

Lee Ralph. More modern parks such as Whakatane are of a world-class standard.

Due to the rural nature of the country, street skating is restricted to the larger cities such as Auckland and Wellington, but the scenes there are still surprisingly strong.

Skateboarding in South Africa is even more laid back than in other places. The hot climate, coupled with the volatile political situation, make skating both a way of easing tension and an activity that requires enormous effort.

Some of the best street spots can be found in downtown Johannesburg, but the atmosphere on the streets is often too dangerous to go skating unless you are part of a large group. This obviously makes it difficult for younger kids who are trying to learn to skate—their only options are to travel to one of the few metal parks around the country, or ride in the shopping malls of the wealthier suburbs.

Elsewhere, Durban has a mellow scene based along the beach front: skating here is very different from what you might find in New York or London, for instance. The lack of stress and pressure makes it more fun in many ways, though, and magazines like *Blunt* and *Revolution* epitomize this attitude.

A skatepark called Boogaloos, often checked out by visiting pros, is a key part of the scene in South Africa. They hold a few contests a year there, where much amazing skateboarding (and partying) take place.

Japan

SKATEBOARDING has grown more fashionable in Japan over recent years. By the late 1990s, Japanese skate companies had started advertising in American magazines. It was not just the appeal of wearing American brands that drew in the millions of yen—the rebelliousness associated with skateboarding held a great attraction for disaffected youth. While schools and colleges stuck to the strict discipline for which they were famous, the real world of work no longer provided the guarantee of a lifetime's career. Homeless people began sharing the streets with skateboarders for the first time: the young found themselves with more time on their hands and a greater appreciation of all things rebellious.

With the growth in skateboarding came organizations like the All-Japan Skateboard Association (AJSA) which runs all the main contests. Several events take place every year at the numerous skateparks dotted around the country, such as Kyushu, B7 or the more recently built Converse park. Amateur skaters earn points for their placement on the circuit at the end of the year, and can turn pro (in Japan at least) if they score highly enough. The world-wide tradition of groups of skaters traveling to contests continues in Japan—cars or vans are hired out, and hot summers are spent camping beside the bowls or ramps in each town.

Most skating takes place in central and southern Japan. Cities such as Tokyo, Osaka, Nagoya and Fukuoka provide the smoothest streets and best architecture—the north of the country is too cold and mountainous.

The Far East Skateboard Network (FESN) produces videos on a regular basis, and magazines like *Fine* and *Ollie* cover all the skating and related events on a nationwide scale.

ABOVE:

MORGAN CAMPBELL, K-GRIND

RIGHT:

CLINT PETERSON, 50-50 KICKFLIP OUT

Shin Okada was one of Japan's best skaters in the late 1990s, with Yush Kawamoto a more recently exported talent, but the skate heritage can be traced all the way back to Shogu Kubo, a 1970s skater who moved to the States and became one of the infamous Z-Boys.

The authorities in Japan are known for a unique anti-skate device: portable rubber mats. These mats have been appearing at some of the best street spots across Japan, pinned down to the ground and rendering the area useless. It's a shame, though, that the authorities rarely provide alternative locations for skating—that is left to commercial companies. New parks are often built by local shops or larger skate companies—even drinks giant UCC has helped with funding in the past.

Europe

SKATEBOARDING in Great Britain has remained strong since the 1970s. A large number of parks were built at the time, both commercial and public, and many of them still remain today, often hidden away in woodland or wasteland. Without the same insurance liabilities that US organizations have had to worry about, councils in Britain left the parks alone when the sport went underground in the early 1980s. In fact, one of the best parks in the world, the Iain Urquhart-designed Livingston Skatepark in Scotland, only opened in 1981.

Competitions were organized by the English and Scottish Skateboarding Associations (ESA and SSA) in places such as Kelvingrove, Livingston, Knebworth, Andover and Kidderminster.

Meanwhile, Welsh skaters kept their surfing connections strong with several ramps in South Wales: Mumbles, West Cross, Cardiff and finally a world-class ramp in Morfa Stadium built after a long campaign by skaters such as Skin Phillips.

A group of London skaters known as LSD (London Skates Dominates) ruled the early scene in the South East. Skateparks on the outskirts of the city such as Romford and Harrow were complemented further into town by constructions in Westbourne Park (Meanwhile I and II), two different parks in Brixton, bowls in Kentish Town, New Cross and Kennington, many of which still remain to this day.

Slalom and downhill skaters had to be more imaginative in their search for suitable locations—on several occasions, contests were held in places as diverse as the pedestrian tunnels to the London Underground station in South Kensington and the Brands Hatch motor racing track. Older skaters like Mark Munns still keep the slalom scene alive in villages like Minety, Wiltshire.

The most famous vert ramps of the 1980s were those in Farnborough, Crystal Palace and later Latimer Road. Often visited by traveling pros like the Bones Brigade, these ramps saw legendary sessions throughout the decade, with riders like Rodga Harvey, Steve Douglas, Bod Boyle, Lucian Hendricks, Neil Danns, Danny Webster and Sean Goff.

Underneath the Royal Festival Hall next to the River Thames lay the South Bank, the spiritual home of English

skateboarding. This arrangement of banks and steps has been the longest-lasting skate spot in the country. Rumors of its imminent demise began around 1988, but the place was still being sessioned in the early 2000s. The long-delayed Millennium redevelopment remains the biggest threat to this skateboarding heartland.

Britain has had various competing magazines: *Skateboard!* in the late 1970s and early 1990s, *RAD* (Read And Destroy) magazine from the late 1980s to the mid-1990s, *Sidewalk Surfer* since the mid-1990s and *Document* since the late 1990s. The magazines have always striven to cover local scenes in detail and have often helped talented skaters from the smaller towns and villages to get noticed.

Skating took off again in Britain after two important events held in London in 1987: the Wind and Surf show, held at Alexandra Palace, and Holeshot, held at the Sobell Center.

Both events brought a host of visiting Americans such as Eric Dressen, Christian Hosoi, Jeff Grosso and Mark Gonzales, who ended up influencing the growing British skate scene a great deal. With the transformation of street skating in the 1990s came a host of new names such as Alex Moul, Simon Evans and later Danny Wainwright and the legendary Tom Penny. By the end of the decade, skaters like Geoff Rowley,

Vaughan Baker, Mike Manzoori, Mark Channer, Colin Kennedy, John Rattray, Paul Shier, Howard Cooke, Frank Stephens, Brian Sumner, Ali Cairns, Spencer Edwards and many more were making a name for themselves in the international world of skateboarding. Following in the footsteps of Deathbox, which later became Flip and relocated to California, British companies such as Unabomber, Panic, Blueprint and Reaction began to gain worldwide recognition.

Skating in Britain has often been a battle with the elements. The most natural reaction to this has been to build numerous indoor ramps and parks, such as Chris Ince's Radlands park in Northampton, which hosted the British Championships through most of the late 1990s. However, the more modern cities of the country will still find their streets plundered every dry evening and weekend available, due to the skaters' endless desire to find new spots—a process made easy by continual redevelopment in many populated areas.

Skateboarding in other European countries has been almost as widespread as in the UK, particularly in France and Germany.

In the 1970s, France had at least two concrete parks in Paris alone—La Villette and Betron Hurlant. These are long gone now, but throughout the country there have been numerous replacements. The South of France

features modern concrete parks in Montpellier and Marseille, the latter remaining one of the best concrete parks in the world. The warmer weather in France has allowed at least two outdoor skate camps to exist, in Bourges and Blagnac. The Blagnac park featured an amazing miniramp complex, street course and vert ramp, but unfortunately was dismantled at the end of the 1990s.

Street skating has continued to remain a popular activity, especially in Paris, which features smooth streets and some of the most skateable modern architecture.

The transitioned concrete pond underneath the Eiffel Tower was famed throughout the skateboarding world in the 1980s and early 1990s. Filled with water most of the time, it was very occasionally emptied for cleaning, and the skaters took over. These dry periods often only lasted a matter of days before the water was piped back in, resulting in feverish and hectic sessions. This spot can be seen in parts of the Blind Video *Video Days*, but today is permanently unskateable as it has been filled with gravel.

French magazines like *Skate France International*, *Zoom*, *Skate* and *B-Side* have provided coverage over the years. Nowadays, skaters like Stephane Larance, Jeremy Daclin and Marc Haziza are showing the rest of the world the talent that exists in France.

The German skate industry owes a lot to the promoter Titus, who has organized national and world championships in Germany since the early 1980s.

In the 1980s, a popular German children's TV show featured the adventures of a young skateboarder and his friends, riding around and challenging each other in some of the skateparks of the time. But there were not too many concrete parks left by the end of the 1990s, except for the well-designed bowl and snake-run in Münster, as well as a few others. Skate stars from the 1980s included Claus Grabke and Ralph Middendorf, both of whom gave their names to pro models from US companies.

Skaters from around the world continue to converge on Münster for the world championships each summer. This traveling entourage often causes mayhem in the town, and each year varying degrees of trouble are quelled by the local police. Everyone from the skaters to the promoters, and from the police to local skinheads are blamed for the problems, which worsened at the end of the 1990s, even making the international newspapers. The 1999 championship was moved to nearby Dortmund, where it has remained since.

Skateboarding in places like Spain and Italy is perhaps slightly less developed, although the skaters are no

less enthusiastic. An excellent new concrete park was built in Seville in Spain in the 1990s, as well as a fiberglass park in Lerida. Older parks around Madrid and in other parts of the country have been sessioned for many years, while the abundance of marble has ensured that Barcelona is probably the world's best city for street skating. Thousands of skaters make the pilgrimage each summer just to sample the city's modern architecture and smooth streets. Spanish skateboarding has been covered by the magazine *Tres 60 Skate*, while Italy's *XXX* has showcased local talent for a number of years.

Most of the good skateparks in Scandinavia have been built indoors, for weather-reasons, especially in Finland to the North. By 2000, many Scandinavian skaters had made an international name for themselves. Ali Boulala, Pontus Alv and Mattias Ringström from Sweden, Rune Glifberg from Denmark and Arto Saari and Harri Puuponen from Finland, all continued to prove themselves in world championship competitions.

Nordic skate magazines have included *Väggarna*, *Funsport*, *Daredevil*, *Edge*, *Numero* and several others. They continue to cover up-and-coming skaters, and leave no doubt that the next generation of Scandinavian youth will have an international impact yet again.

Colin McKay

ALONG with Danny Way, Colin McKay has pushed the technical side of vert skating more than anyone else. His sections in the first two *Plan B* videos showed some tricks many skaters couldn't even understand, let alone do. Switchstance moves were combined with flip tricks in a way that pushed vert skating forward once again, and probably boosted its resurgence in the mid-1990s.

Bob Burnquist

BRAZILIAN skater Bob Burnquist has only been on the international scene since around 1995, but in that short time he has had a profound effect on vert skating. Just when everyone was beginning to think that all the tricks had already been invented, he came along and invented a whole load more, and took switchstance skating to outrageous levels. Sometimes taking complete contest runs in switch, which were better than most could ever do normally, he showed the vert skating world just how far it could really be taken, and inspired thousands of street skaters to try vert skating in the process.

Skate Culture

FROM THE VERY BEGINNING, SKATEBOARDERS HAVE MADE THEIR OWN CULTURE. NOT JUST WITH CLOTHING AND WAY OF LIFE, BUT WITH A DIFFERENT ATTITUDE TO THE WORLD AROUND THEM. SKATERS LEARN TO SEE NORMAL THINGS FROM ALTERNATIVE VIEWPOINTS AND THE RESULTING CULTURE HAS PROVED TO BE HIGHLY INFLUENTIAL IN THE NORMAL WORLD.

DEPT. OF HOUSING

ANY PERSON NOT BEING A
RESIDENT OR GUEST OF A
RESIDENT, FOUND IN OR
UPON THESE PREMISES
WITHOUT LAWFUL EXCUSE
WILL BE PROSECUTED BY
VIRTUE OF THE ENCLOSED
LANDS PROTECTION
ACT 1901

Music and Skateboarding

BY the late 1980s, skateboarding was associated with bands such as Suicidal Tendencies, Anthrax, INXS and Faith No More, although some had more integrity than others. The Beastie Boys used skating on stage during some of their earlier appearances, and mentioned skating in various lyrics at the time.

Since then, they have maintained a close relationship with the skate industry, built a ramp in their studio, and later worked with acclaimed video director Spike Jonze.

Skaters taking part in contests used to choose the music to be played during their run. This was often a way of showing their individuality, as well as hoping that their favorite music would help them skate better. Bands such as Slayer remained a popular choice, but as the 1980s turned into the 1990s hip-hop and dance music began to be represented more often. The same has been the case with video parts: back when skate videos were much less frequently produced, the choice of music to go with a skater's section often proved crucial.

Bands such as Operation Ivy increased their sales dramatically when their tracks were included in various H-Street videos. Since that time, every genre from classical to country to Japanese noise has been used in skate videos, while skaters also continue to make the music themselves. Paulo Diaz had exceptional talent in both skating and music throughout the 1990s and often played rare tribal instruments in his video sections. Physics, the wheel company, produced a video with music made entirely by the skaters on the team, and included a free CD of the tracks too.

As we step further into the 21st century, skaters and music continue to be closely linked. Skateboarding is once again used as a marketing tool by various record companies. Some of the biggest summer music festivals around the world regularly feature skate contests or demos as part of their line-ups. Clubs from Los Angeles to London have installed mini-ramps to be used by those for whom dance music isn't exhilarating enough, and even teen pop idols have used skateboarding to increase their street credibility. As skateboarding carries on being used in this way, perhaps it's time skateboarders stepped back and took a look at the potential damage to the integrity of the sport. Maybe it's time to start up those punk bands once again.

PREVIOUS:
**CASWELL BERRY,
FEEBLE GRIND**

BELOW:
**TOSH TOWNEND
5-0 GRIND**

ABOVE:
**STEVE OLSEN
360 FLIP**

Natas Kaupas

IF PEOPLE remember Natas Kaupas for one thing, it will be his legendary ollies over trashcans in the Santa Cruz video *Wheels of Fire*. But he was also breaking ground in many other areas of skating, such as wallrides and kickflips, as well as style and attitude. Like Mark Gonzales, Natas (pictured right, with Jim Rose) had a unique eye for skating and took new tricks to street furniture that had never been used before such as fire hydrants. His incredible talents were certainly recognized at the time: he was given the first-ever skateboard signature shoe with Etnies in the early 1990s.

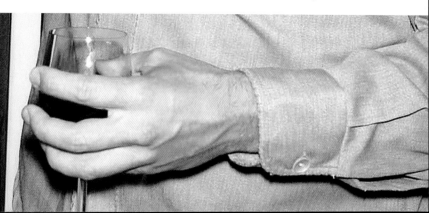

skateboard teams of the time. Their shoes are developed in the intriguing Sole Technology Institute: a research facility where skaters perform tricks while motion-capture equipment and pressure pads measure various physical forces at play. The data is used to develop shoe technology, helping protect riders' feet from the rigors of modern skate tricks.

Surf and snowboard companies have made attempts to promote skate clothing with varying degrees of success. To Joe Public, who often seems unable to differentiate between skating, surfing and snowboarding, these clothes seemed highly desirable—but skaters have often held back from providing mass support. The most successful technique appears to have been the creation by these businesses of new, skate-specific brands, thus cutting visible links with other sports to gain credibility in the notoriously sceptical skate world.

As skaters inadvertently continue to create popular fashions, they remain intrinsically aware of corporate interest and will not hesitate to turn their backs on anyone who begins to sell out.

In response, many skaters will raid thrift stores and charity shops for more unique items, and will sometimes do anything to avoid wearing a skate-related logo. At the end of the day, it's the skateboarding itself that matters and younger skaters would do well to spend more on equipment and less on T-shirts.

THIS SPREAD:

MATT HENSLEY
KICKFLIP GRAB

Skateboard Art and Artists

THE creative abilities of skaters have often been turned toward art, especially since the first board graphics started appearing in the 1970s. Early pioneers included Wes Humpston and Craig Stecyk, who developed the first board graphics for Dogtown Skates around 1978. A few years later, Vernon Court Johnson began producing some of the most popular graphics of all-time for Powell Peralta. Working with skulls, snakes and dragons to produce stickers and T-shirts as well as board graphics, Vernon almost single-handedly created the most memorable images of the biggest skate company of the 1980s. At the same time Jim Phillips was producing a gruesome cartoonish style for rival company Santa Cruz; his skate artwork featured in the 1994 retrospective *The Skate Art of Jim Phillips*.

As skateboarding picked up again, so the graphical style became more innovative and informal than the more traditionally artistic work of before.

Mark Gonzales and Neil Blender were two influential skaters who would often doodle on their griptape, later going on to design their own graphics for their pro models.

Neil Blender helped to start up Alien Workshop, whose imagery proved incredibly popular in the mid-1990s, and he also painted an album cover for the band Dinosaur Jr. Mark Gonzales had a unique artistic style which was validated further in 1998 when two books of his fiction were published. To coincide with the release of this work, *Broken Poems*, Mark took part in a unique promotion in Europe.

Wearing a fencing outfit, he skated randomly around a German museum

to the bemusement of many fans and onlookers, before attending readings and signings over the next couple of days. Since then Mark has continued to produce art, including 1000 limited edition sculptures for the music label MoWax, and continued to skate professionally for Krooked skateboards.

Andy Howell, was a pro skater and talented artist of the early 1990s, producing some highly stylized graphics for New Deal and later Element, as well

ABOVE:
BOARDS ON DISPLAY

RIGHT:
COLIN KENNEDY, SWITCH 5–0

as clothing company Zero Sophisto. Ed Templeton, another New Deal rider at the time, has since gone on to become an influential artist and graphic designer in the industry. He created the unique identity of Toy Machine in the late 1990s, whilst successfully showing his artwork in world-renowned galleries. Marc McKee was, at the same time, producing some stunning and sometimes controversial deck graphics for the World Industries stable of companies.

Ex-Bones Brigade member Lance Mountain founded his skate company The Firm in the early 1990s. An accomplished photographer as well as artist and skateboarder, Lance has created a distinct individuality with the company, producing a friendlier aesthetic than a lot of skateboarding imagery in the process, perhaps reflecting the warmth of the proudly religious team.

The appeal of Japanese animation led pro skater Jeremy Klein to use some of the imagery for board graphics, T-shirts and stickers in the early 1990s. The incredible popularity of the designs, which were introduced a few years before Japanese Manga and animation had begun to be widely accepted in the US, paved the way for Jeremy to set up the company Hook Ups, which later produced Japanese-influenced clothing and shoes. Since that time, both

ABOVE:
MODERN BOARD GRAPHICS

LEFT:
**JAMIE THOMAS,
FRONTSIDE BOARDSLIDE**

Japanese and American artists have been commissioned to produce graphics in the Manga style for a number of skate-oriented businesses.

As skateboarding matured, so different companies' decks became more similar in shape and construction, and graphics began to be the major selling point. In the 1980s, pro graphics often stayed the same for a year or two, particularly with the big-selling decks such as the Vision Gator and Powell Peralta Tony Hawk models. But as skateboarding entered the 1990s and a host of new, smaller companies split up the industry, so the turnover and importance of graphics increased. All sorts of gimmicks were tried to entice skaters to purchase—decks with velvet glued into the design, lottery card-style, scratch-off graphics, free packs of stickers to place on pre-designed deck

scenery, physically scorched-on imagery, hand-painted graphics and controversial scenes of sex or violence.

Some of these met with more success than others, but as the industry went into recession, wood shops began to produce blank boards with no graphics at all which could be sold at a much cheaper retail price.

While these may have saved skaters valuable dollars they caused untold damage to the industry itself, ruining brand identities and upsetting the pro model system, as well as causing problems for skaters when these anonymous decks broke or wore out too quickly. In a rare moment of collaboration, the industry decided to dramatically reduce the number of blank decks available, and once again poured funding into pro models and the graphical identities associated with them.

Danny Way

DANNY WAY shot to fame in his teenage years after beating Tony Hawk in a legendary Add-A-Trick contest. One of the few skaters to be influential on street as well as vert, he took the technical side of street skating onto vert ramps, inventing tricks like the Kickflip-Indy, and pioneering lip maneuvers such as Ollie Blunt variations. As one of the tiny handful of skaters to have been serious about landing tricks like the 900, his confidence and determination became apparent in the late 1990s, when he broke the world record for the highest air on a skateboard and jumped out of a helicopter into the ramp on the same day. In 2003 he again smashed the world records for both longest and highest airs, flying around on his especially built Mega Ramp.

ABOVE:
**KEENAN MILTON,
SWITCH FRONTSIDE NOSESLIDE**

RIGHT:
**MATT MUMFORD,
BACKSIDE LIPSLIDE**

LEFT:
**DANNY WAY,
METHOD AIR**

Skateboard Contests: Not an Olympic Ideal

SKATING has always been about seeing what you could do on a skateboard, where you could do it and how well it could be done, so the development of contests comes as no surprise.

Skateboarders enjoy pushing each other to the limit, testing themselves and overcoming fears; that's all part of the fun of the sport—although the word 'sport' is far from ideal, as I hope you are beginning to understand.

The first skate contest was held in a high school in California in 1963. As the years progressed, disciplines such as high jump, long jump, 360s, slalom and freestyle came to be introduced. With the exception of freestyle, which required the opinion of a judge as to who was the best skater, each of these events was very easily measured, either with a stopwatch, a measuring tape or a counter. Perhaps this is why some organizers were so optimistic about skateboarding becoming an Olympic sport in 1984—the sport was also becoming highly organized and corporate involvement was the norm. The increase in the rebellious nature of skateboarding at the end of the 1970s helped to put an end to this dream, and also affected the running of skateboard contests themselves.

Traditionally, the skateboard contest has been a fun event, too. Organization is kept to a bare minimum, since skaters dislike filling out endless forms, wearing numbers and skating at exact times.

There are no rules as to what tricks should or shouldn't be done, no official points system, and the events are often just excuses for skaters to meet and skate with each other. However, this anarchic contest style has been changing over the years, with the increase in prize funds available, frequent television coverage and, once again, corporate involvement.

Since the mid-1980s the World Cup in Münster (later Dortmund), Germany, has been the biggest contest in the skateboarding calendar. The prize money has grown over the years, and entrants have frequently come from places as diverse as Brazil, Israel, Japan and Scotland. Skaters from around the world who could only afford to travel to one

ABOVE:
ERIC KOSTON
AT THE X GAMES

RIGHT:
SASHA STEINHORST
IN SHANGHAI

contest each year, began to choose the German World Cup over events held in the States. This added to the truly global flavor of these events, and increased the prestige of winning the championship. By the early 1990s, the contest focused on the two most popular disciplines in skating: street and vert, dropping freestyle in 1992.

It would be a travesty to mention skateboard contests without mentioning Tony Hawk. Tony has won more skate

contests than any other skater alive, taking nearly every important vert title from his first win in 1982 right up into the late 1990s and beyond. This incredible feat has only occurred through a huge amount of time, effort, dedication and self-discipline from the California-based Birdhouse pro.

Tony's father Frank Hawk also provided great support from the beginning, and from its inception in 1982 ran the National Skateboarding Association (NSA), which organized amateur and professional contests throughout the decade.

Another memorable contest skater was the freestyler Rodney Mullen, who was only beaten once in competition, by Swede Per Welinder in 1983.

Street skating contests have seen fewer consistent winners over the years, perhaps because of the rapid development of the discipline and its greater accessibility to younger skaters.

In 1995 an uncomfortable change emerged on the contest circuit. US television network ESPN hosted the Extreme Games, an event featuring skateboarding among several other 'extreme' sports such as in-line skating and BMX riding. MTV followed with similar events a few years later, and these televized occasions marked a distinct alteration in the organization of skate contests, with an outside body making many of the decisions.

Compromises were also made with the design of the street course: it had to accommodate in-liners and BMX riders as well as skateboarders, and initially it seemed skateboarders suffered the most from this. Since then the ESPN format has been improved considerably, more skateboarders have a direct involvement in design and organization and the annual events are gaining some respect within the industry.

By the end of the 1990s, the World Cup Skateboarding (WCS) organization was running most big contests, with many amateur events put on by Vans, the California Amateur Skateboard League (CASL) and numerous independent distributors and organizations.

Brian Schaeffer's Skate Park of Tampa (SPOT) ran popular amateur contests throughout from the early 1990s onwards. Corporate involvement was kept to a minimum and the ramps were constantly updated and redesigned, which helped attract a large number of professional and amateur skaters to regular events in Florida.

When snowboarding made it into the 1998 Winter Olympics in Nagano, Japan, many skaters were keen to see what effect it would have on the sport. Within snowboarding itself, certain top pros boycotted the event entirely, while others took it as seriously as regular athletes. With allegations of drug-taking and unsportsmanlike behavior rampant,

element began to reappear in the contest world: girl skaters. Patty Segovia organised the first All-Girl Skate Jam in 1997, and later events featured over 100 female skaters competing in street, mini ramp and vert events.

The most famous girl skater during that period, and a true heroine to many girl skaters around the globe, was Elissa Steamer. She not only entered (and won) various girls-only events, but was talented enough to enter several regular contests as the only female participant and still place respectably. Other prominent girl skaters at the time included Jamie Reyes, Carabeth Burnside, Jen O'Brien, Jaime Erickson, Heidi Fitzgerald and Vanessa Torres who all followed the groundbreaking stars of the 1970s and 1980s such as Ellen Oneal, Vicki Vickers, Anita Tennesohn and Lori Rigsby.

Since the 1970s, various world records have been attempted on skateboards. Often during major contests, records such as the number of 360s completed or the long jump, as won by Tony Alva in 1977 with a leap over 17 barrels, were set and recorded. More dangerously, skaters have tried to achieve the fastest speed on a skateboard (perhaps up to 90 mph), which in recent years has been facilitated by the extensive development of the luge skateboard.

British skater Danny Wainwright holds the record for the world's highest ollie, at 44.5 inches. On vert ramps, the highest air has been recorded regularly since the early 1980s. Steve Caballero held the record for a period during the 1980s, but in 1997 all previous records were smashed by vert legend Danny Way, who used a specially-built ramp to achieve a height of 16-and-a-half feet above the lip. Many pundits thought this record would stand for years, but Danny himself destroyed it and many other records in 2003 after the building of his Mega Ramp. Using this enormous construction, he managed to jump an amazing 75 feet across a gap, and fly 23.5 feet straight up into the air.

snowboarding was seen as the black sheep of the Olympics. It is important to remember that even snowboarding already had far more of an official judging system than skateboarding, and perhaps that reason alone will keep skating out of the Olympics for the foreseeable future.

Meanwhile, organizations such as the WCS were beginning to impose stricter categories on skateboarders for contest entry. In the late 1990s, the WCS published a set of clear guidelines defining 'professional' and 'amateur' skaters.

In the years prior to that point many amateurs had caused a fuss by entering pro contests and placing highly, or sometimes even winning, so it was clear something had to be done. Perhaps the

companies themselves were to blame, though: many skaters remained pro long after their best days were over, simply because their name and reputation continued to sell decks, while talented newcomers were experiencing difficulty finding themselves sponsors.

However, this debate remains an uncomfortable one within the industry; reputations must be built in order to sell any decks at all, yet a line must be drawn somewhere between capitalism and greed. One of the key issues is the very short length of time skaters can remain at their peak; depending on their lifestyle and attitude this can be anything from a year upwards. Pro skaters remaining at the cutting edge for several years are very rare indeed.

In the late 1990s, a very positive

ABOVE:

BAM MARGERA, OLLIE OUT OF PARK

LEFT:

CAWELL BERRY, HEELFLIP

Authority and Rebellion

SKATEBOARDERS have long been thought of as rebels, for various reasons. On one level, many skaters are adolescent males who will get labeled as rebels no matter what they do, whether it is skateboarding, playing in a band or just hanging out. On another level skaters do use the urban environment in a way in which it was not designed, and this often provokes a negative response from members of the public. It's a natural response —what they don't understand must inherently be bad—and it's a predictable response, too. Most skaters who've sessioned a city square or a schoolyard have experienced a reaction of this kind. Accused of everything from simply being a nuisance to committing a federal offense, the imagination of the accusers knows no bounds. Rarely are they wise enough to see what an innocent activity is really taking place, or to see some of the much worse alternatives presented to modern teenagers. But skaters put up with it as always, and will not hesitate to answer back their accusers in the same language used at them. That obviously creates another rebellious image.

What amuses those who look at the long-term situation is the following: those teenagers from the 1950s and 1960s who were considered so rebellious at the time are often the ones so outraged at the activity of the skaters 20 or 30 years later, as if skateboarding has suddenly become truly harmful compared to the innocent fun that they had in their youth.

It has to be said that there is another level within skateboarding that does present itself as truly rebellious on

ABOVE:
ELISSA STEAMER, OLLIE

RIGHT:
STEVE BERRA, K-GRIND

purpose. Taking their cue from the punk scene, many skaters adopt a semi-anarchic approach to life, where causing trouble is a well-respected activity. Again, this is a common thread with a lot of kids, and while frowned upon by many, it is actually a surprisingly positive outlook in the longer term.

The more intelligent troublemakers will always realize that rebellion is a catalyst for change. Any stagnant system or organization will need rebels to break ranks in order for progress to take place. History has proven this over and over again, yet few understand how important progress is in the development of a species. Some humans have a tendency toward order and organization, while others do their best to destroy that to make way for the future. The two have always balanced each other out quite nicely, so an eradication of all things rebellious would certainly spell doom for this finely tuned set-up.

The law in many countries has often decided to frown on skateboarding. Even open-minded Scandinavian countries clamped down in the 1970s, and some Communist countries banned the sport entirely because of its association with the United States. Today one would think that things were far less political than that. Well, perhaps not.

Politicians, police and lawmakers who make decisions such as banning skating often have just one simple agenda: to increase votes and/or funding for themselves, so a new law banning skateboarding in a downtown district, for instance, is seen by many as a step to reduce crime; and with the crime-rate being a major preoccupation with most authorities, such a law may help win the expected votes or funding. The public, who know little better, congratulate the move with enthusiasm and appear to attempt to kid themselves that drug-dealing and violent crimes will be reduced as a result.

The skaters will simply move on, often made more keen by the new challenge presented to them, because

skateboarding is essentially about personal challenge—often it just gets confused with rebellion, that's all.

One of the main problems with the rebellious image associated with skating is the fact that innocent young skaters get tarnished with the same brush as real street criminals. While kids are arrested for skateboarding and brought home in tears by over-zealous cops, violent crimes are being committed just blocks away. As the real criminals pose a greater physical threat to the police, perhaps busting a couple of 12-year-old skaters seems a far more tempting 'crime-fighting' tactic on one of

those coffee-and-doughnut afternoons. Cops like these should spend time in countries like Ecuador or Brazil and learn the necessity of catching proper lawbreakers.

In the meantime, all skaters can do is respect those who confront them, and perhaps even shock them with politeness. Slightly devious tactics like this are far more effective than mouthing off or getting physical, and subsequently they may even convince authorities that skaters are indeed human, and perhaps deserve public facilities after all. That way we may all get to skate the streets and the skateparks.

ABOVE:
**COLT CANNON,
HEEL FLIP**

RIGHT:
**JAKE RUPP,
180**

The Nomadic Way: Couch Skating from City to City

ONE of the best and worst things about skateboarding is the amount of traveling involved. It remains a dream for unsponsored skaters to travel the world performing demos, entering contests and visiting skateparks, while for many pros actually doing it can be hugely tiring and stressful. Pros are often expected to perform at their best after a 12-hour flight, poor food, in a foreign country, so it's no wonder they might prefer to stay at home. The amount of traveling also means that sometimes college or school must be compromised, and families or partners are not seen for months at a time. A new generation of sponsored skaters such as Ryan Sheckler, Leo Romero and Zered Bassett chose home schooling over regular attendance, in order to allow them to skate more both at home and on tour.

Fortunately, most young skaters end up appreciating travel; it's always eye-opening and not many people in their teens or 20s get to travel the world so cheaply or freely.

Even for unsponsored kids, travel remains an important part of skateboarding. Most countries have contests that are held throughout the year and they provide an opportunity for skaters to pile in the back of a van or get on a bus and have a long weekend away.

While the peers of many teenage skaters are to be found moaning about their surroundings in Hicksville, skaters are usually more resourceful people who will save up the pennies, scrape up some transport and meet up with friends, pros and amateurs, at events held a few hundred miles away. These treks are an important experience as far as learning

THIS PAGE:
**JAMIE THOMAS,
360 FLIP**

independence goes, and they are something that parents should support in any way they can.

Since the main industry is based in California, many skaters have embarked on an even bigger adventure. From all over the States, and even the world, confident skaters have taken the plunge and moved out to the West Coast, not knowing where they are going to stay or for how long. This brave move sometimes results in a miserable homecoming a couple of weeks later; but just occasionally skaters hook up with the right people, prove their talents in a short period of time and may even become established pros in the long term. Either way, it is certainly a courageous decision to make, and definitely not necessary if you are a particularly talented skater—the industry will always find you in time.

Traveling skaters have sometimes earned a bad reputation in the towns and cities they visit. If you imagine what it's like to be cooped up in the back of a van for three days before stumbling out into a backwater town you will never visit again, it comes as no surprise that skaters have to let off steam in some way. Of course, the smaller the town is, the more likely it is that locals will take offense to the attitude of visiting skaters, or that the skaters themselves might end up being more imaginative in their search for entertainment. Needless to say, skaters do actually get kicked out of some strait-laced hotels, while rock stars just seem to boast about it.

Another reason that travel is so important to skaters is to do with the way skaters see the world. Skaters make mental maps of places according to skate spots, and will often ignore geographical boundaries or distance. For instance, it's a fair bet that many skaters from all over the US know more about the excellent benches in Barcelona's Plaza de Cants or the smooth inclines on the South Bank of London's River Thames than they do about La Sagrada Familia or St Paul's Cathedral. Likewise, on a more local level, towns and cities are divided according to the smoothness of the streets or the abundance of skate-able architecture. The better the skate spot, the further skaters will travel to skate it, from Livingston Skatepark in Scotland to legendary ditches in Hawaii. The most disused quarter of a faded industrial city may end up with a wealth of skate spots, and skaters will not hesitate to travel to it. Their agenda is not economic or social: it is purely functional.

want is people being noisy or loud or having public demonstrations... or even people being quiet and playing chess or reading books. What they actually want is a very homogenous idea of city spaces. A lot of people have got to the point now where they kind of think, 'OK, perhaps we want things that aren't planned'; but what they haven't worked out is that those non-planned things might be different to the things that they want. The one thing that I don't think planners are very good at is planning for difference as well as for spontaneity.

JD: That's to our advantage, of course.

IB: Well I'm not sure, if all urban squares were designed in order that skateboarders could use them as well, would skateboarders be very interested in that? Because it seems to me that the whole point about skateboarding, to some extent, is that you are not supposed to be doing it. There's a strong counter-cultural element to it—a notion where you've got to have something that's not liked. That helps frame skateboarding sub-culture; the whole idea of identifying what it's not. I think that what people are trying to do is... not trying to control skate-boarding, they're trying to control disorder. I saw one of your other questions, about whether skateboarding is a form of vandalism: well, OK, it might scratch a few things, but if you compare it with the damage a car does, it's absolutely ridiculous. So why are people complaining about skateboarding? Well, they're not complaining because it really causes damage, they're complaining about it because it disturbs their sense of normality. Skateboarding is untidy. It doesn't do what it's supposed to do in the places and the times for which functions are allotted, so therefore people are opposed to it.

RIGHT:
STACEY COWERY, HYDRANT OLLIE

FAR RIGHT:
BENNY FAIRFAX NOLLIE HEELFLIP

BELOW:
JAMES CRAIG, NOSEBLUNTSLIDE

4

Skateboarding Media

MAGAZINES ARE PROBABLY THE GREATEST RECORD OF THE HISTORY OF SKATEBOARDING; EACH PERFECTLY CAPTURES THE MOMENT IN SKATEBOARDING IN WHICH IT IS CREATED. AS THE SPORT DEVELOPED, SO DID THE IMPORTANCE OF MAGAZINES AND THE SKILLS OF THE PHOTOGRAPHERS AND WRITERS WHO MADE THEM. WHAT MAKES THE SKATE MAGAZINES UNIQUE IS THAT THEY ARE ALMOST UNIVERSALLY CREATED BY SKATEBOARDERS THEMSELVES; THE SKILLS OF WRITING AND PHOTOGRAPHY ARE LEARNED EITHER ON THE JOB OR IN THE STAFF'S SPARE TIME. THIS HAS NOT MEANT SHODDILY PUT-TOGETHER PRODUCTIONS, THOUGH, IN FACT IT HAS BEEN QUITE THE OPPOSITE. SKATEBOARDING MAGAZINES ARE RENOWNED FOR THEIR INNOVATIVE STANDARDS IN BOTH PHOTOGRAPHY AND DESIGN.

Magazines

BY the early 2000s, skate magazines were very popular, selling tens or hundreds of thousands of units per issue around the world, and the skateboard media had become an industry in itself. Large publishing houses now own several skateboarding titles because they are seen as a commodity just like many other magazines, from sports to women's magazines.

In most cases, skate magazines have kept true to their roots; showcasing up-and-coming skaters as well as established stars; providing world-wide contest coverage and discussing all the various developments, rumors and ups and downs of the industry. There are now several skateboarding-specific titles in many developed countries as well as a considerable number of other magazines that either occasionally or regularly discuss skating.

In the 1960s, *Surf Guide* began to include articles about the new sport of skateboarding, but the first magazine entirely dedicated to skating was *The Quarterly Skateboarder*, first published in 1965. Lasting only for four issues, the title returned ten years later as *Skateboarder*, and was renamed again as *Action Now* in 1980, when skateboarding was dying its second death.

A key title no longer in existence is *Poweredge*, which lasted for part of the third phase of skateboarding in the late 1980s.

The oldest magazine still in operation, *Thrasher*, which began in 1981, has continued to champion its own independent attitude. The magazine has consistently provided skaters with interesting articles and viewpoints, as well as photography of a tremendous variety of skaters and skate spots from all around the world.

Transworld Skateboarding began in 1983, in response to the rapidly

widening market of potential readers. With the agenda of appealing to a much wider readership than *Thrasher* magazine, *Transworld Skateboarding* has succeeded in showing some of the most stunning photography, the most innovative graphic design and articles from countless different countries.

Movie director Spike Jonze began his career as a photographer on *Transworld* while influential graphic artist David Carson also helped define the magazine's identity.

Big Brother began in 1992, and quickly caused a rethink amongst certain other publications. The innovative marketing gimmicks, controversial attitude and lack of censorship helped the magazine become a success, although many shops were hesitant to carry it and some television stations even ran stories about its supposedly damaging effect on kids. Dave Carnie took the helm and wrote brilliantly with irrelevant irreverence about everything from cat shows to religion. The magazine was part of pornographer Larry Flynt's stable until early 2004, when it ceased publication.

Slap magazine also began in 1992. Though not achieving the sales of other magazines, *Slap* has continued to provide readers with another alternative outlook on skateboarding. With quality photography, writing and design, the magazine has kept an edge of integrity compared to some of the other titles.

Skateboarder magazine returned in the 1990s in an annual collector's issue format and then again in 1999 as a fully fledged title. In 2003, the newest magazine, *The Skateboard Mag,* entered a volatile market.

One of the few titles produced outside the US to receive widespread distribution was *Sidewalk Surfer*, based in the UK.

Formed from the ashes of *RAD* magazine, *Sidewalk* sells all over Europe and parts of the US with its distinctive photography and attitude, and regular coverage of the skate stars of tomorrow.

Skate Videos

SINCE the 1980s, videos have become an essential product from most skate companies.

The big-budget, film stock productions of the 1980s became threatened in the next decade, as it seemed as if anyone with a cheap video camera was beginning to produce their own skate videos. While the new videos allowed younger skaters to be showcased and rare spots to be uncovered, they also ended up undermining the importance of new video releases. What had been a major event just a few times a year had turned into a tiresome overload of weak productions released several times a month. Large premieres were not bothered with, production values were low and brands became diluted. Only in the late 1990s did companies realize once again the importance of reducing the quantity and increasing the quality of video productions. Quality film stock began to be used again and budgets rose, to the benefit of all concerned.

The Powell Peralta videos from 1984 onward set new standards all round. As well as featuring some of the best skating ever seen, they included humor and good direction. Powell Peralta's third video, *The Search for Animal Chin*, centered around a story involving a global quest to find the legendary skater Animal Chin. While the story was not feature-quality, the skating and overall style of the production made it one of the best skate videos of all time. Their next two videos, *Public Domain* and *Ban This*, featured amazing footage of some of the best street skaters of all time, such as Frankie Hill, Chet Thomas, Ray Barbee, Guy Mariano, Paulo Diaz, Rudy Johnson and Mike Vallely.

The other company making big budget productions in the late 1980s was Santa Cruz, especially with its videos *Wheels of Fire* and *Streets on Fire*.

No one who saw it at the time will forget Natas Kaupas' incredible section in the first video. The second production featured a story-line about pro skater Jason Jessee being sent to death row for skateboarding.

The first batch of videos to eschew the big budgets of the previous years in favor of more raw skate footage included the H-Street videos *Shackle Me Not* and *Hocus Pocus*. Sections from skaters like Danny Way, Matt Hensley and Sean Sheffey have ensured that these titles have gone down in skate folklore.

ABOVE:
**SEAN SHEFFEY,
50-50**

New Deal and World Industries produced videos with a more lo-fi aesthetic at this time too, but still managed to keep the standard of skating high.

Widely regarded as one of the best skate videos of all time, if not the very best, is the first Blind production, *Video Days*. Mark Gonzales and Spike Jonze helped to put together an atmospheric and memorable production, featuring the most talented street skaters including Guy Mariano, Rudy Johnson, Jason Lee and Mark Gonzales himself. Ending with a dramatic auto-wreck off a cliff, the video ensured each skater's name became etched in stone.

With the progress of skateboarding in the early 1990s came a host of new companies and videos. Plan B's *Questionable* and *Virtual Reality* were among the first to document massive handrail skating from the likes of Pat Duffy and Danny Way, as well as featuring pro freestyler Rodney Mullen applying his skills to the streets, and numerous other talented skaters such as Mike Carrol, Rick Howard and Colin McKay.

Spike Jonze returned to work with Girl, and produced their two videos, *Goldfish* and *Mouse*, both of which were memorable for their use of humorous interludes as well as skating and featured definitive sections from many of the 1990s' top skaters, including Eric Koston.

As skating went back to basics in the mid-to-late 1990s, simpler tricks were taken higher and further than ever before. Videos such as Toy Machine's *Welcome to Hell*, Zero's *Thrill of It All* and *Misled Youth* pushed the boundaries of handrail and gap skating further than ever.

A consequence of this was that the slam sections traditionally featured in most videos became much more dramatic, often featuring cracked limbs and other horrific injuries.

Videos had begun to diversify in order to cover the widening scope of skateboarding, and the major skate magazines all produced videos to cover these different styles.

A video-only magazine, *411*, had become well established by this point, providing bi-monthly updates, contest coverage, advertisements and features on new and established stars from many different sponsors.

By the early 2000s, skate videos were once again becoming carefully conceived productions. Some featured short films, others focused only on teaching new tricks; interludes were frequently more artistic and the budgets went up again.

ABOVE:
**AARON ROWE,
FRONTSIDE NOSEGRIND**

The Birdhouse production, *The End*, cost hundreds of thousands of dollars to produce and was shot entirely on film stock. It included a specially built ramp for Tony Hawk to perform the loop and some of the best skateboarding ever seen from the other team riders, Rick McCrank, Andrew Reynolds, Willy Santos, Steve Berra, Heath Kirchart, Jeremy Klein and Bucky Lasek.

This long-overdue return to the methods used in the first Powell Peralta videos was welcomed by the industry, and helped skate videos in general to regain some of their earlier prestige.

PJ Ladd's *Wonderful Horrible Life* showcased a relatively unknown group of US skaters, not least the massively inspiring PJ Ladd, whose unique way of smoothly linking tricks together has influenced a new generation.

Flip's *Sorry* was finally released after probably the longest period in gestation by any skate video: perhaps about eight years, depending on who you ask. It featured long-awaited sections from Bastien Salabanzi, Geoff Rowley and Tom Penny amongst others.

Interview with Mike Manzoori

MIKE MANZOORI is an ex-professional skateboarder who now works as a well-respected videographer. Here he tells us about how he got started in the industry, and how the impact of new digital technologies is affecting the nature of skateboarding.

JD: What were you doing in the States before that?

MM: For the last few years before I've been concentrating on making skate videos for a company called Sole Technology, and they handle eS, Emerica and Etnies footwear, so I've just been doing all the video production for them, whilst trying to skateboard as much as possible.

JD: How's the skating going as you get older?

MM: I've had some pretty heavy back injuries for the last four years so for me it's kind of stunted everything. I stopped skating professionally a few years back to concentrate on the video side of stuff.

JD: Did you always think you'd end up doing something like that?

MM: I didn't really plan on it, it just kind of fell into place. I'd spent so much time involved with skateboarding—more than anything else in my life—most of the people I knew were through skateboarding, so it just kind of seemed to be easier to get a job with the people I knew, and

people actually started offering me jobs as opposed to me looking for them, which is quite handy.

JD: What was the first video you did, *Jello*?

MM: Yeah, that was just a laugh. I happened to have a video camera 'cos Santa Cruz—who I was sponsored by at the time—sent me one so I could get footage. Mat Fowler was finishing his college project, which was to design the whole graphic look of a skateboard company. For fun we thought we'd enhance his end of year show with a video as part of the presentation for this fictitious company. So it was me and Mat and Mark (Channer) who had access to the media department, and we went out one weekend and did the whole video that weekend. Since then I've just been doing it for fun, until eventually it became my job.

JD: Doing it in a weekend is pretty impressive, especially compared to what goes on today.

MM: These days you'd be lucky to get a 30-second ad done in a weekend. These things take so long now, because there's just so much that has been done, and people have seen it all before. People are not only one-upping themselves in what they do, they are one-upping the next guy on the next page in the magazine, or the next video. There's a lot more to compare yourself to these days, which is why kids just do the same trick down two more stairs or a longer gap, or if someone does one trick then they'll do it switch.

JD: I think your videos seem to be able to tap into the creative side that represents the feeling of what it's like to go skating, rather than the work ethic of one-upmanship.

MM: It's the more artistic and free side of things, rather than the sporty, athletic

BELOW:
MIKE MANZOORI IN MANCHESTER, ENGLAND

JD: How about with tricks? It's been quite a while since there's been any real innovation on the trick front.

MM: That's true. These days it's got to the point where if you boil down a new video, there are only about five minutes of really new or interesting stuff. Even the cutting-edge videos, you just get the feeling that you've seen so much of it before. It's hard to be original because there's millions more skaters these days, but not millions more tricks.

JD: I'm amazed at the standard of 10–12 year old kids today, it's so high.

MM: It used to be that if kids were doing those kind of tricks you knew exactly who they were and where they'd come from and all about them because there was only a few of them. It's a weird thing.

JD: On the other side of the coin, it's great to see films like *Dogtown* come out, that represent the history, so these kids can see where they've come from.

MM: I thought *Dogtown* was pretty damn good. It went to a way wider audience than just skateboarders, so it had to explain things a certain way, framing things more generally so the Average Joe would understand it. It's also good because it's another thing that makes skateboarding more accessible, but it can fuel the tendency people have of thinking skateboarders are just rebellious punks. I think *Stoked* was really good due to the way it portrays what goes on with all the money that's available; that you can tour the world and have what you want, but the movie is able to show that the whole dream is very superficial. That it doesn't last forever and you've got to take everything with a huge pinch of salt. It puts things into the perspective that it's not all glamorous rock'n'roll, that the bubble could burst at any point. Not just you as a skater, but the whole industry—companies, shops and so on—is constantly teetering on the edge.

side of it. It's the difference between a hobby or a passion as opposed to a goal that you're working towards.

JD: It's amazing how you get all these pro skaters whose career-oriented way of skating involves waiting for the photographer or videographer, then driving an hour to a single spot to do a single trick.

MM: It's all very staged. Everything is overshadowed by the glamor of multiple flashes and generators. But you can make just as good a video by pushing around the streets with a camcorder with your buddies; it doesn't have to be a huge production. If there isn't any essence there, then no matter how nice you make it look it's not going to be appealing.

ABOVE:
**KRIS MARKOVICH,
OLLIE OVER TRASH CAN**

JD: It could be though that skating was always going to be on this level if it was going to be successful. Perhaps the earlier, more underground days of skating will be looked back on as the anomaly, like the times when you went up to go and speak to someone in the street just because they had a pair of Vans on.

MM: Pretty drastic things like that have changed for sure, but I'm always worried that I'll seem like the old guy. A kid getting into skating now is going to see just as much magic as we did, but just in a different way to before. They're going to get different stuff out of it, and that goes way beyond just the world of skateboarding; they are used to so many more stimulating things these days.

JD: It's made me think of how you do need something of an attitude to be a certain type of skater though. If you are lining up for a trick where you either land it or go to hospital, that requires a particular mentality. A willingness to suffer for perhaps much greater reward.

MM: That's true, but also take when we were young: for anyone to kickflip down any set of stairs, however small, was pretty shocking, but now you've seen them do it down twenty stairs, or sixteen or whatever. As soon as that was landed, as soon as it got to that stage and people could see it in magazines and videos, then everyone's like, 'Well, that's done now. We don't have to do that or see that or think of that anymore'. You get all these insane vaults and leaps, and as soon as it's captured on video then it's the job done, and it can be put to rest. This has bred a whole bunch of skaters who live for these magic moments that come and go. A lot of skaters are genuinely good, but a lot get sponsored and appear to be good, but they can't actually skate around between these magic moments. I'm not saying everyone should be able to slash a bowl and do an invert, but push around a little, you know what I mean? Look comfortable on your skateboard.

JD: What about the affect of video-games? It seems to have changed expectations of what's possible on a skateboard. The Tony Hawk games seem to have quite an affect in influencing a younger generation to believe that a lot of the crazy moves available in the games are actually possible. If you think that a ridiculous move is possible then you may not actually achieve it, but you might get halfway, which is still a leap forward that was previously unimaginable.

MM: They are definitely stretching the boundaries, I totally agree. One of the craziest things about these video-games is that they've made the rest of the world know what skate tricks are called. You'll be trying a trick on the street and some random dude will come up and go 'Aren't you gonna 360 Japan air that?' It's kind of bizarre in that respect. But the more kids think is possible, the more will be possible. I remember as the 1980s turned into the 1990s, there were magazine articles that looked back on the last ten years and tried to predict the next ten years. They were pretty close but no one expected what was really going to happen, and you never really can.

JD: I'm always wondering what the next thing is going to be, whether it'll be a new type of trick, or a new fashion or whatever. The DVD thing is pretty good actually, that seems to be having some affect on skateboarding itself.

MM: Yeah it is a really good format for skateboarding. The way you put together a skate video, there is so much emphasis on a rider's part that a lot of stuff gets overlooked simply because it's not suitable for the rider's part. Hours of footage ends up getting put aside simply because it's not part-worthy, or because it doesn't fit in with the stock skate video structure: the intro montage, the rider's parts and so on. So we tried to do something different with the *Emerica* DVD; tons of footage of Heath throwing his board around and stuff. It gives the whole format a little boost, allows you to be a little more experimental. Also, skaters tend to watch a video all the way through for only the first couple of times, then they just want to cut to the chase of their favourite part, which they can now do at the touch of a button. You can stick on old media, information about the company, old photos and so on, just ram it full of media for the kids to chew on. When I was 13 or 14, I didn't want to look at schoolbooks, I wanted to look at skate mags and videos; if today's stuff was available to me I would have been pretty hyped.

JD: Do you think this will affect the way videos are made from the point where you've got the camera, and perhaps the skating as well?

MM: As something is being filmed I know where it's going to end up. One of the good things about skate videos is there tends to be only one or two

people in charge of the production, from the creative filming and editing side of it, so it's easy to carry ideas through right from the concept—which can often be there in the field when it happens—because the same person is doing the filming, and the logging, and the editing and the music, and the graphics for the DVD. You couldn't really do it any other way with skateboarding. The bigger the production the more heads are involved.

JD: What sort of budget do videos have these days?

MM: More money than it's worth! *eS* video cost over half a million dollars to make; *Emerica* video is not much short of that. That includes production and travel and all kinds of expenses. The biggest cost, though, comes from the fact that it takes years to get done; the footage that you get from those two years of filming doesn't all go in to the video, some goes to commercials and promos and lots of different offshoot areas. Some of the time, the first six months of filming that you thought were going to go in the video part, well, by the end of year two you've already progressed so much that that's old hat,

which is where it might become DVD bonus stuff.

JD: Why do videos take so long to create these days?

MM: They take longer and longer because people take longer to get better, at least in comparison to the standard of skating between videos. If you were to chart it in a graph, you could say that skaters have this really steep learning curve at first, then it arcs out after a while, where it takes much longer to learn more tricks. Usually you're going to get sponsored right where the graph is at its steepest; you get media attention while things are really good, and then by the time skaters are into their second and third video part, a few years into their career, it's going to take about two years to get something really new or worthwhile. Also because they've built up this reputation that they can't step back from: you've always got to be one better than yourself. Take Terry Kennedy, I think he was sponsored and pro after skating for just a couple of years, which is good: he does some pretty gnarly stuff. It all depends on what you're exposed to, who you're around,

what your opportunities are; if you're some kid in a rainy part of Bradford in the north of England, you're not going to get to skate the spots or skate with the people. Things aren't going to happen as easy for you. But the good thing is those kids are often the diehards; they are the super-versatile skaters.

JD: The weather does seem to have an affect, like with the differences between West and East Coast skaters in the US.

MM: Well, for some people these factors can be a hindrance, for others it just makes them even more driven. When they do skate, they make the most of the fact that it might only be two or three times a week, as opposed to a sunny day every day, that's what gives them the extra drive.

JD: If only you could switch that energy on at any time.

MM: Well, sometimes you try and turn it on artificially when you're filming or shooting photos. I guess with filming you can't get away with it so much: these days batteries last for ever, and if it's your job, like me, you're not supposed to only

THIS SPREAD:
**GUY MARIANO,
SWITCH POP SHOVE IT**

have one tape on you. But the photographer can still say 'Last try' or something like that, so the skater can usually pull their finger out and get on with it. Saying that, the photographers are going digital now, which is good because the skater can try harder stuff. I've seen photographers go away with a shopping bag full of used film on a single sequence, literally 50-100 rolls. It's great for the environment that we don't have to do that anymore, but it's also interesting because skaters can be put more at ease when they are trying harder tricks for the camera as they are not quite as driven to make stuff. It will mean that you'll see harder stuff as sequences but it will also mean that they'll probably take a lot longer to make them.

JD: It's weird to imagine that technology could have an effect on skateboarding like that.

MM: Well, these days a lot of pro skaters have laptops with copies of their footage on it and they make their own versions of their video part.

JD: But isn't that a problematic idea? Surely most pros are better at skating than at video editing?

MM: Well, Andrew Reynolds pretty much edited his own video part for the *Emerica* video, we just refined the editing a little bit. He knows what he wants and he does a pretty good job. But then there's other skaters, who I won't name, who really shouldn't touch the editing part, and should just stick to what they are good at.

JD: I guess it happens in other areas too. There seems to be a trend towards skateboarders producing different types of creative output, not all of which is necessarily good. Plenty of skaters paint or play guitar or write poetry or whatever, but perhaps they shouldn't always inflict so much of this on the world at large. It seems inappropriate that a pro is able to

leverage his celebrity into churning out paintings if he's not a good artist.

MM: I know what you mean. It's weird when people start making offshoot careers just because they were good at skateboarding. There's quite a large breed of skate artists who if they didn't ride a skateboard would never stand as strong artists, they would never be having exhibitions; they'd be told to go back to college and learn properly.

JD: Perhaps where it comes from is that skateboarding is very specifically about the self: the pain you have to experience

ABOVE:
**ARTO SAARI,
BLUNT TRANSFER**

and the focus you have to achieve make successful skateboarding quite a selfish activity. It's not really a team sport.

MM: It's weird. Skaters can be really individualist, and really sheep-like at the same time. They are the most individual team I've ever seen. The different styles and looks of skateboarding are just teams, in a way.

JD: Lots of people being alternative together. Not really a great difference between that and football, is there?

MM: Well, there is more freedom. Boil it down to just skating down the street: you choose where you weave in and out of people, there's no right way or wrong way up and down the road for you, the lines on the road don't apply to you. Literally everything is broken down and you're in charge of your environment as well as yourself which I think is what makes it so catchy to kids. With skateboarding it's nice because once you get over the fundamental rules of balance and the physics of it all, then you start to learn how to bend those rules. You've got yourself to roll along and levitate for a split second and it makes you feel pretty good.

JD: There's the skater's eye that you get as well. The way of seeing your surroundings is certainly an enlightening experience, the way you begin to negotiate shapes and surfaces and textures in the city so they become more real for you.

MM: It's pure interaction; the way you can embrace these things. You even start looking at your own body differently too. Most people fall and take a scrape and lose some skin, even the hardest skaters can't say that that stuff doesn't hurt, whether it's the first or five hundredth time, it bloody hurts. You start seeing the worth in trading that off, the buzz is so strong that it makes you come back for more.

Skateboarding and the Movies

THE changing popularity of skating has often made it a subject for the movies. Sometimes skating is included as part of an action sequence; at other times it is an integral part of the plot. While it does showcase the sport to a mainstream audience, skateboarding sections are often poorly directed and leave many skaters laughing or cringeing.

Skater Dater was a short film from the 1960s, and was probably the first production to feature skateboarding. It wasn't until the 1970s that film-makers began to really get their teeth into the sport, and some more memorable films were made. Surf film-makers were the first to catch on, and included skate sequences in pictures like *Five Summer Stories*, *Super Session* and *Hard Waves/Soft Wheels*.

The two skateboard-only features of the time, *Freewheelin'* and *Skateboard*, featured pros such as Tony Alva and Stacy Peralta alongside regular actors, in stories written especially to display skate action sequences.

Magic Rolling Board was another short film of the 1970s; shown before main features like *Rollerball*, it included skating from all over the globe.

Jackie Chan's film, *Wheels on Meals*, is interesting because it contains a few short sequences of him skateboarding. The tricks he does are pretty basic, but it's fascinating to watch the control he had on a board; all coming from a stunt background.

Hollywood lost interest in skating when it went underground. It was 1985 before the next important film to include skating came along. *Back to the Future* featured Michael J. Fox's character street-skating in the early part of the film.

The short segment proved to be massively influential, and thousands of skaters around the world will testify today that it was the moment they first decided to get a board.

In 1986 came another movie which featured skating heavily, *Thrashin'*. The story of two rival skate gangs did little to convince theater-goers, or indeed skate-boarders, to see the film in droves, even though it included skaters such as Christian Hosoi and Lance Mountain.

The late 1980s saw *Police Academy IV: Citizens on Patrol* and *Daredreamer* incorporate skateboarding, but it was *Gleaming the Cube* from 1989 that put

ABOVE:
BRETT MARGERIETAS, FRONTSIDE LIPSLIDE

real effort into basing a story around the sport. It featured Tony Hawk and Rodney Mullen alongside Christian Slater. The dramatic but unrealistic ending of the film left many skaters disappointed.

The Skateboard Kid, from 1994, is the most obvious attempt to base a feature film solely on skateboarding. The story of a boy's adventures with his mysterious and magical board, the movie featured skating from pros Josh Beagle and Willy Santos. The director could have done more to include spectacular sequences: there are almost as many bails in the film as there are tricks landed.

In 1995 came one of the most controversial films of the decade, *Kids*. Written by Harmony Korine and directed by Larry Clark, the story simply includes skaters as the main characters rather than focusing on skating itself. Most of the roles were simply acted by skaters themselves, and in homage to the Blind video *Video Days,* one sequence sees a bunch of skaters chilling out and watching it together.

2001 saw the release of *Dogtown and Z Boys*—Stacey Peralta's documentary about the legendary skate team from 1970s Los Angeles—which ushered in a new era of mainstream understanding and appreciation of skateboarding. Narrated by Sean Penn, the movie tells of the team's heavy influence on modern skateboarding, from their rebellious ways to their emphasis on style.

In 2002 a darker tale was unveiled. *Stoked: The Rise and Fall of Gator*, directed by Helen Stickler, told how ex-pro Mark Rogowski was convicted of murder in the early 90s. This depressing documentary revealed how the excesses of the pro lifestyle could add to the woes of a disturbed mind, with fatal consequences. *Rollin' Thru The Decades*, a British documentary, was released in 2004.

Directed by skater Winstan Whitter, it celebrates British skateboarding's spiritual home on London's South Bank, and brings some stylish nostalgia to this previously untold story.

Digital Skateboarding

SKATEBOARDING has featured in a large number of video games since the 1980s. Many companies have attempted to cash in on the rebellious nature of the sport as an alternative to regular sports games such as football or ice-hockey.

One of the first games, and still one of the best, was *Atari Games' 720* from 1986. The player controlled a skater who cruised around a town visiting four different skateparks, each representing a different discipline of the sport. The classic nature of the game was confirmed in 1999 when it was converted and released for Nintendo's Color Game Boy. Other early titles included the *Skate or Die* series from Konami. Appearing on several different formats, these games achieved considerable success at the time, but remain less playable by modern standards.

As the 'extreme' bandwagon began to gather steam, so a number of games were produced featuring skating among other sports. Sony PlayStation had at least three compilation games made for it in the 1990s, but the best skateboarding game in the arcade was to come from one of its rivals, Sega. In 1997, *Top Skater* appeared in the arcades, and proved to be an addictive playing experience. Realistic and fantastic tricks were combined, and graphically sumptuous environments provided the backdrops.

The most exciting console skateboarding game came in 1999, from Activision. *Tony Hawk Pro Skater* for PlayStation allowed the player to choose from real-life skaters such as Chad Muska, Jamie Thomas, Andrew Reynolds and Bob Burnquist. Street spots and skateparks from all over the US were digitally recreated for the game, and the player could simply skate around learning new tricks if they wished to. This game sparked a host of sequels and imitations, such as games sponsored by *Thrasher* or

ABOVE:
TONY HAWK'S PRO SKATER

MTV, until 2004, when a crowded market was beginning to tire of skate games, and developers took titles online in order to further extend play possibilities.

With the expansion of the Internet in the late 1990s, skate companies began to use the medium as yet another tool to promote their products and team riders. But even during the 1980s, *Thrasher* magazine in the US and *RAD* magazine in the UK were communicating online with their readers. The earliest discussion groups about skateboarding also began during this decade, long before the advent of the World Wide Web in 1990.

The explosion of the Web in the mid-1990s brought with it countless new sites dedicated to skateboarding. Some were produced by kids in backwater towns to show photos of their friends in the local spots, while others were fully-fledged, online catalogues from major skate companies, shops and distributors. Since then, numerous sites have developed. There is no doubt that the use of the Internet is set to increase in the skate industry. There is little point in discussing particular skate-related sites; new ones come online all the time, while others are best forgotten. The best tip is to look for yourself at your favorite company's website and check out the links from there.

Saying that, the best thing to do really is to turn your computer off, quit playing games, and go skateboarding.

Do it now.

Matt Hensley

MATT HENSLEY stormed the world of skateboarding with his part in the H-Street video *Shackle Me Not* from 1988. His fresh approach to street skating—a combination of newer technical moves like *Kickflip* and *No-Comply* variations—boosted the enthusiasm of a younger generation. Matt went on to become one of the top pros, and subsequently proved a major influence on the top pros of 10 years later. When he went into semi-retirement in 1992, the skateboard world mourned his absence; but by the late 1990s he was skating once again and playing an important part in the industry, as well as playing accordion for the acclaimed band, Flogging Molly.

THIS SPREAD:
**RUDY JOHNSON,
SWITCH 180 OLLIE
LOS ANGELES**

Tricks and Techniques

BELOW:

KARL WATSON,
KICKFLIP

STANDING ON A BOARD

When you first stand on a skateboard you've got to find out which way you skate—goofy or regular. Goofy is with the right foot forward and regular is with the left foot forward. The best thing is to just roll around a little bit and see which way seems more comfortable for you. It's best to try and learn both ways if you can—the hardest way for you is called switchstance skating.

TURNING

With you knees slightly bent, simply lean in the direction you want to turn in, and your trucks will do the rest. The two directions in which you can turn are called frontside and backside; with a frontside turn your front faces outwards, and with a backside turn your back faces outwards.

PUSHING

With your weight towards the front, place your back foot on the ground at the side of the skateboard in front of you. Now push hard against the ground with that foot, and you should be propelled forwards. Quickly put your foot back on the board, and away you go.

STOPPING

You can just jump off to stop at first, but be careful when you land. Dragging your feet is another more controlled technique. Take your back foot off the board and lower it towards the ground as if for pushing. As it makes contact, bring your weight slightly back onto the dragging foot, and increase the drag until you slow down and stop. The most commonly used technique is the hardest, but quickest, method of stopping: sliding. Begin to lean as if for a frontside turn. With you body leaning slightly backwards, you have to do two things at once. First of all, 'unweight', which means that you need to make yourself lighter by jumping slightly without leaving the ground, and then push the back of the board hard and forwards so that it is 90 degrees from where it started. When it

reaches that point, you should be pushing, and sliding, with equal force on both the front and back wheels. Once perfected, you can stop in a very short space if you need to.

THE KICKTURN

With one foot firmly on the tail and the other above the front truck, lean back to lift the nose of the board into the air, whilst pivoting around at the same time. At first just try and turn a few degrees, later you'll be able to do 180 and 360 degree turns.

THE ACID DROP

This involves riding your skateboard off a small drop, but a good place to learn it is a local curb. Skate straight towards the edge at a moderate speed, and as the nose of your board approaches the edge, raise the front truck as you would for a kickturn. When your back wheels ride over the edge you will begin to fall towards the ground. Keep your weight centered and absorb the landing when it comes.

THE OLLIE

This move is the basis of almost every street trick today. Begin with your back foot firmly on the edge of the tail with the ball of the foot centered. Your front foot should be around halfway up the board, or perhaps further forward; experiment to find what's best for you. Bend down to get some spring in your legs, and then you have to do several things at once:. without leaning back, put all your weight on your back foot and jump into the air—this will make the board go near vertical. To counteract this, and to get the board to stick to your feet, you need to drag your front foot to the nose of the board and level your feet out at the peak of the jump. This should all happen within a split second, but it takes hours of practice, so be patient. Anyway, that's the hardest part; once you're in the air with the skateboard stuck to your feet, gently push it back down to the ground and compress your legs when you land.

Guy Mariano

GUY MARIANO has often kept out of the limelight since his influential skating of the early 1990s. An incredibly talented skater, he has done countless switchstance tricks that most skaters will normally never achieve. One of the few skaters who really pushed what was possible on a skateboard well into the 1990s, photos and video clips of Mariano are rare and often classic.

Use the same technique to learn nollies (nose ollies), switch ollies and fakie ollies (backwards ollies).

RAMP SKATING

First of all, you're going to have to be able to push, stop, kickturn and skate backwards before you even get near a ramp. Once on a ramp, start from the flat bottom, and ride up and down the ramp a little. As you get more confident, start using your weight to push against the curve of the ramp, this is called pumping and it will help you gain momentum. When you are pumping up and down with ease, it's time to try kickturns. Just keep crouched down, and kickturn through 180 degrees when you reach your peak. Grinding is the next stage,

and at first it is just like a kickturn, except that you do it at the highest point possible on the ramp. Learn both frontside and backside grinds at the same time, if you can.

THE DROP IN

Begin by placing your board at the top of a small bank or ramp. The tail should sit on the platform and the rest of the board should be hanging over the obstacle. With your back foot on the tail and your front foot over the front truck, crouch down slightly and start to lean forward. You have to lean forward with your shoulders and when it feels like all your weight is right over the slope, push down with your front foot and ride away. You should try this move

ABOVE:
**JAMIE THOMAS,
FRONTSIDE FEEBLE**

on smaller obstacles first. Dropping in on huge vertical ramps is something plenty of skaters will never do.

THE ROCK FAKIE

Once you have learned all the previous moves, ride up with enough speed to reach the lip with ease. Place the center of your board on the coping and bring your weight halfway onto the platform to rock the board over. When you're ready, bring your weight back into the ramp, and then rock the board back in using a pivoting motion and the back wheels. If you dropped in to a rock fakie, try and return to the other lip in a drop in position. Simply go through the drop-in process in reverse as you approach the lip.

Tom Penny

TOM PENNY comes from Oxford, England. He raised the standards in the US skate scene in the mid-1990s as a rider on the Flip team, but for several years previously he had been virtually worshipped in the UK as one of the most talented skaters of all time. There is little point in trying to describe how good he is at skateboarding, or attempting to sum up his unique and refreshing attitude to the pro lifestyle. His story is full of mystery and intrigue, and helps to keep his name whispered in the highest circles. Needless to say, he keeps his head fairly low nowadays (hanging out in France or Argentina), and he remains many influential pros' favorite skateboarder of all-time. Long live Tom Penny.

RESPECT...

MAGAZINES

100% Skateboarding (UK); *Big Brother* (US); *Big Issue* (UK); *Document* (UK); *Edge* (Sweden); *Funsport* (Sweden); *Numero* (Finland); *Phat* (UK); *Poweredge* (US); *RAD* (UK); *Sidewalk Surfer* (UK); *SK8 Action* (UK); *Skateboard!* (UK); *Skateboarder* (US); *Slap* (US); *Thrasher* (US); *Transworld Skateboarding* (US); *Tribo* (Brazil); *Warp* (US)

BOOKS

Bastard, Harry. *Spots: A Guide to Rideable UK Architecture*. WJ&T, Brighton, 2001
Blake, John. *The Complete Guide to Skateboarding*. Phoebus Publishing Co. London, 1977
Borden, Iain. *Skateboarding, Space and the City*. Berg, Oxford. 2001
Brooke, Michael. *The Concrete Wave*. Warwick Publishing, Toronto, 1999
Gonzales, Mark. *Broken Poems*. Tropen Verlag, Cologne, 1998
Gonzales, Mark. *Social Problem*. Little More, Tokyo, 1998
Hawk, Tony. *Occupation: Skateboarder*. Harper Collins, 2000
Hills, Gavin. *Street Skating*. Wayland, Hove, 1992
Irrgang, Sebastian. *The Do-Tank*. RCA, 2004
Mackey, Jan. *Sydney for Kids*. Horan, Wall and Walker, Sydney, 1982
Marsh, James. *Activators: Skateboarding*. Hodder Children's Books, London, 1998
Polhemus, Ted. *Street Style*. Thames and Hudson, London, 1994
Rose, Aaron. *Dysfunctional*. Booth-Clibborn Editions, London, 1999
Weyland, Jocko. *The Answer is Never: A History and Memoir of Skateboarding*. 2002

ACKNOWLEDGEMENTS

Many thanks to Mike Manzoori and Iain Borden for sparing the time to be interviewed, to Legends on Oxford Street, London, and to all others who assisted with the creation of this book, especially Phyllis, Carol, Alan and Louise.

PICTURES

All pictures kindly supplied by Skin Phillips except for:
70, 94, (Carlton Books Ltd); 10 (Time Life Pictures/Getty Images); 58 (Jamie Squire/Getty Images); 76 (Elsa/Getty Images); 77 (Stanley Chou/Getty Images); 65, (Alex Oliveira/Rex Features).
Screen grabs on page 104 from *Tony Hawk Pro Skater/Activision*, photos by Rosie Matheson.